Praise for *CALM for Moms*

T0049984

"All moms worry. It can feel so natural and so important, moms don't always know there is another way. Denise Marek has found the perfect formula to normalize this worry as she gently reassures and guides the reader toward comfort with evidence-based strategies for relief. *CALM for Moms* is a perfect companion and should accompany every mother coming home with a new baby!"

—Karen Kleiman, founding director of The Postpartum Stress Center and author of *Good Moms Have Scary Thoughts*

"*CALM for Moms* is just what parents need to help us worry less and, as a result, parent our kids better. Our worry can be contagious since our kids feel the ramifications of our stress. The better we manage our worry, the more our kids will benefit! Denise Marek's four-step, research-based plan is practical and user-friendly; her helpful ideas can be practiced immediately. This new book is full of real-life anecdotes and an easy-to-follow step-by-step guide to help you worry less and enjoy your life and parenting more fully and happily. I recommend this book to all of the worriers out there who are ready to take control and charge of their mind and self-improve!"

—Cynthia C. Muchnick, MA, co-author of *The Parent Compass: Navigating Your Teen's Wellness and Academic Journey in Today's Competitive World*

Published by Familius LLC, www.familius.com
PO Box 1249, Reedley, CA 93654

Familius books are available at special discounts for bulk purchases, whether for
sales promotions or for family or corporate use. For more information, contact
Familius Sales at orders@familius.com.

Library of Congress Control Number: 2022942213

Print ISBN 978-1-64170-732-9
Ebook ISBN 978-1-64170-790-9

Printed in the United States of America

Edited by Tina Hawley, Sarah Echard, and Spencer Skeen
Cover design by Carlos Guerrero
Book design by Brooke Jorden

10 9 8 7 6 5 4 3 2 1

First Edition

CALM
for moms

FAMILIUS

To Lindsay and Brianna

CONTENT WARNING

The CALM process was born out of necessity for me: it grew out of my personal struggles and experiences. It has reduced my worry and anxiety and has also helped thousands of people who have attended my workshops, read my books, or completed my online courses to do the same. However, in describing the CALM process, it is necessary for me to write about some true but difficult events in my life: depression (Chapter 7), alcoholism in the home (Chapter 15), and disordered eating (Chapters 15 and 19). Reading about these events may be triggering for some.

I also want to make it clear that in no way do I want this book to substitute for the care of a medical professional. If you are experiencing any physical or mental health issues, please consult with a medical professional for comprehensive care.

Contents

Mama Bear, when you're feeling worried, read this book. It contains your complete four-step process to transform worry into inner peace. This step-by-step process has already helped thousands of people around the world to stop worrying.

You picked up this book looking for results, strategies, and steps you can easily implement to stop worrying and connect with your inner peace. You'll find exactly what you're looking for right here, so you've made the right choice! Congratulations on taking that first step into your new worry-free life.

The Gift of Worry-Free Parenting

Learning how to transform worry into calm isn't just a gift for you. It's also a gift you can pass along to your children. As L. R. Knost wrote, "When little people are overwhelmed by big emotions, it's our job to share our calm, not join their chaos."[1] The challenge is that you can only share what you possess. With the CALM process, you'll gain strategies to find calm in the chaos and transform worry into inner peace. You can then put an end to the worry cycle in your family and share your calm with your young children, teenage children, adult children, and even grandchildren.

Note that this is not a parenting book; I won't be giving advice on how to parent your children. Instead, this is a book for moms *who worry*, a book that will teach you this simple, effective, and parent-tested four-step process to reduce stress and worry and give you the tools necessary to enjoy a happier, more present parenting experience.

While I've centered this book on moms and their experiences with worry in the context of motherhood, many of the ideas in this book can be adapted to apply to anyone who parents and is looking for ways to reduce stress and worry.

But before we begin transforming the worry you've been feeling into the inner peace you desire, here are a few points to remember.

First, You Can Stop Worrying!

No matter how much you've worried in the past or even how much you're worrying right now, you can stop worrying. I know you can, because I did—and let me tell you, I was once one of the biggest worriers on the planet. I worried about my kids and what other people thought of me; I worried about money and my relationship. Was I lovable, likeable, or good enough? You name it, I worried about it. In fact, my mom used to say to me, "Denise, if there was nothing in the world to worry about, *you* would find something."

Constant worry prevented me from enjoying the early years of parenting my two daughters. It wasn't until I was in my late twenties and working as a seminar leader for an international business-training company that I learned a way to regain control of my thinking. I ran trainings on topics like "Self-Esteem for Women," "Conflict and Confrontation," "How to Get Rid of Clutter and Organize Your Life," and "Dealing with Difficult People." After about eighteen months of learning these strategies and teaching them to others, I realized I wasn't worrying anymore. I thought, *Wait a minute. If the world's biggest worrier can stop worrying, there's hope for everyone.* So I began to study worry. I started paying attention to how my own thinking had changed, and I created the four-step process you will learn by reading this book.

This four-step process is called the CALM process. *CALM* is an acronym for the four steps to worry-free living:

- ¤ Challenge Your Assumptions
- ¤ Act to Control the Controllable
- ¤ Let Go of the Uncontrollable
- ¤ Master Your Mind

And this process truly works! I've experienced chronic worry firsthand, and I've spent over two decades researching worry and how to get free from its grip. The CALM process worked for me, and it will work for you too. These four steps will help you to

- ¤ break unhealthy thinking habits;
- ¤ reduce the physical effects of stress;
- ¤ learn to find inner peace amidst chaos; and
- ¤ replace negative thoughts with positive declarations.

When you use the CALM process, you'll stop worrying—it's that simple. You've heard of the light at the end of the tunnel. The long tunnel of worry can minimize the light in your life, but CALM contains the steps that will remove that tunnel and finally let you see "the light." And here's the thing about the light: it isn't just at the end of the tunnel. It's all around you right now. Even if you can't see it or feel it, it's there. That's what you're about to experience—the incredible peace and happiness that comes from leaving all of that worry behind you. Living with inner peace *is* possible, and by the end of this book, you'll be experiencing it firsthand.

Second, You Deserve Inner Peace!

You really do deserve inner peace! You deserve to live your best and happiest life. If you've *ever* doubted your value, your worth, your likeability, your lovability, or even your "deserve-ability," you're not alone, but you don't have to keep doubting forever. You can gain freedom from those self-limiting beliefs by following the strategies in this book. In the meantime, know that you really do deserve to live a life filled with inner peace and that such a life is precisely what you'll find in these pages.

Third, You're Exactly Where You Need to Be!

By reading this book, you're on the right path toward worry-free living. The CALM process can help you through some of life's biggest challenges—challenges like depression, addiction, separation, or divorce. CALM is also designed to help you deal with the smaller everyday worries—like anxiety about what other people think of you and fear that you don't measure up as a mom. (By the way, Mama Bear, parenting is tough, and you *do* measure up!) Alongside strategies to deal with those feelings, you'll also read about ways to reduce the stress that comes from mess triggers, noise triggers, and the overwhelm accompanying becoming a mom.

Let's Begin!

You took the first step into your worry-free life by picking up this book, and you made the right choice! My job is to guide you through this proven four-step process, and that's exactly what I'll be doing during our time together in these pages.

CALM for Moms is based on my first book, *CALM: A Proven Four-Step Process Designed Specifically for Women Who Worry.*[2] Similarly to that book, this book is divided into five parts. Parts 1 through 4 each reveal a step in the CALM process. In Part 1, you'll learn how negative assumptions create unnecessary worry, and you'll be given six specific strategies for challenging those assumptions. In Part 2, you'll discover how to use worry as a prompt to take action. You'll also learn how to craft an action plan, overcome fears blocking you from following through, reduce the physical and emotional effects of stress, and execute bold action by making value-based decisions. Part 3 provides strategies for letting go of worries that are beyond your control: worries about the past, the future, and those uncontrollable things in the present. You'll learn how to let go of upset feelings, hurts and offenses, mom-guilt, mom-shaming, perfectionism, and fear. Part 4 outlines techniques to master your mind and guard against negative thinking by planting new, positive thoughts and speaking aloud to restore inner peace. These are vital skills because your inner dialogue largely dictates whether you feel worried or calm.

Finally, Part 5 puts the entire four-step process together. Here you'll find "Transformation Tracking Sheets." These sheets come together to form your personal at-a-glance template to be used anytime worry arises, so that you can reconnect with your inner peace in a snap!

In addition to the tracking sheets, scattered throughout this book are fun and games. You'll find puzzles, fun exercises, jokes, CALM Moms' Glad Libs, and more. These activities have been strategically designed to enhance the lessons, reinforce what you're learning, and sometimes have you laughing out loud. You'll also find real examples from real moms dealing with real issues—just like you. Their stories will give you hope and inspire you. Picking up this book has already started you on your journey toward a more peaceful, joyful, worry-free parenting experience! Let's begin.

PART 1

Challenge Your Assumptions

To let go of worry in a hurry, challenge your assumptions.

I was recently speaking with my twenty-six-year-old daughter, Brianna, about how Amazon keeps track of the most high-lighted books and passages on Kindle e-readers. I had read that one of the most highlighted books on Kindle is the Bible and that the most highlighted passage in that book is "Be anxious for nothing" (Phil. 4:6).

When I discovered this fascinating fact, I asked Brianna, "Why do you think that is? Why do you think 'Be anxious for nothing' is the most highlighted passage?"

She replied, "Oh, that's easy! It's because people are always anxious for no reason."

"Hold on a minute," I said. "Let's back this up a bit. Do you think 'Be anxious for nothing' means 'Oh, go ahead and worry about any old thing for no reason at all'?"

"Yeah," she said. "And I'm always anxious for no reason, so I must be doubly blessed."

We had a good laugh about her interpretation, after I explained what the passage *actually* means: Don't worry about anything.

Can you relate to what my daughter said? Are you feeling doubly blessed by an extra helping of stress? Well, buckle up, Mama Bear, because this first step will help you let go of a great deal of your worry in a hurry. The first step in the CALM process is the letter C: Challenge Your Assumptions.

Human beings are assumption-making machines! You think your infant isn't making enough eye contact? You make assumptions. Your teenager is late getting home? You make assumptions. You compare yourself to other moms on social media? You make assumptions. We all make assumptions. Making assumptions can be a helpful tool for humans to figure out missing pieces and to make sense of what's happening around us. However, when the assumptions you make are *negative* ones, an enormous amount of worry can set in. In fact, most of our concerns are a result of making assumptions about all of the things that *could* go wrong and all of the bad things that *might* happen. Negative assumptions create worry.

You're about to learn six assumption-busting strategies that include a variety of questions you can ask yourself to help challenge your assumptions and restore your inner peace *before* you find yourself feeling "anxious for nothing." But first, let's talk about the stress response itself.

CHAPTER 1

Put the Brakes on the Stress Response

Imagined Danger versus Real Danger

The first week in our new home, in the middle of the night, my bedroom door slammed shut, the sound jolting me awake.

What was that?

My heart was pounding. I could see lights flashing on and off outside my main-floor bedroom window.

That's the alarm!

We had moved to the country, and our alarm consisted of external house lights blinking on and off to alert others. This visual alarm was installed because our closest neighbors lived too far away to hear the beeping of a sound alarm.

Someone broke into the house, I thought. *Oh no! The kids!*

My first impulse was to run upstairs to my daughters' bedroom. But then I thought, *Wait. If the intruder is already upstairs, he could knock me unconscious, and I won't be able to help the girls. Get the dogs!*

I jumped out of bed and ran downstairs to let our two extremely large German shepherds out of the basement. Then I turned around and ran upstairs as fast as my legs would take me. It all happened so quickly, I'm not even sure who made it up the stairs to my daughters' room first—me or the dogs!

I raced upstairs to find both my girls safe and sound asleep. My husband and I then searched the house with the dogs to figure out what had tripped the alarm.

Aha! The back door from the bathroom attached to our bedroom was open. It hadn't been closed properly earlier that day. In the night, the wind had blown it open, which both triggered the alarm and caused an air vacuum to suck our bedroom door shut.

The mystery was solved. The possible threat had passed. We were all safe, and knowing that, my mind and body were able to calm down.

My body's stress response had been triggered, and it gave me the clarity and strength to dive into action. Rest assured, Mama Bear, when you need to protect your family in the face of danger, you will have what it takes to do so! Here's why.

The Science of the Stress Response

There's a part of your brain that always remains alert to danger. It's called the amygdala. The amygdala is responsible for initiating the stress response—also known as the fight-flight-freeze response. The amygdala interprets sounds and images, and when it perceives something as a threat, it sounds the alarm by sending a message to the hypothalamus. When the hypothalamus gets that message from the amygdala, it signals the sympathetic nervous system to hit the gas to give the body the energy it needs to respond to the danger.

What happens when the sympathetic nervous system hits the gas? The adrenal glands (located on the top of each kidney) release epinephrine—a hormone more commonly known as adrenaline—into the bloodstream. Adrenaline then circulates through the body, creating physiological changes: Your heart beats faster than normal to push blood to your muscles, heart, and other vital organs. Your pulse rate speeds up. Your blood pressure goes up. Your breath quickens. The small airways in your lungs open wider to allow the lungs to take in as much oxygen as possible. Your brain becomes more alert with extra oxygen. Your sight, hearing, and other senses become sharper. Blood sugar (glucose) and fats from temporary storage sites are released to supply energy to all parts of your body.

By the way, all of this is happening so fast that your brain's visual centers haven't even had the chance to fully process what you're seeing. It's pretty remarkable. And there's more!

After the initial adrenaline surge, if your brain continues to perceive something as a threat, the hypothalamus activates the second component of the stress response. That second component is called the HPA axis (hypothalamic-pituitary-adrenal axis, to be exact). The HPA axis signals your sympathetic nervous system to keep the "gas pedal" pressed down through a series of hormonal signals. The hypothalamus releases a hormone called CRH (corticotropin-releasing hormone). CRH tells the pituitary gland to release another hormone called ACTH (adrenocorticotropic hormone). ACTH tells the adrenal glands to release yet another hormone called cortisol to keep the body revved up and on high alert.

Once the threat has passed, the parasympathetic nervous system—the part of your nervous system that promotes the rest and digest responses—puts the brakes on the stress response. Cortisol levels fall, and your body begins to calm down. It's an incredible process, and it all begins when the amygdala sounds the alarm indicating a potential threat.

The night my door slammed shut, my amygdala assimilated the information (the sound of the door followed by the visual of the lights flashing on and off outside of my house) and set off a chain reaction of hormones. That's why my heart was pounding. That's why my brain was crystal clear about possible actions to take to protect my family. That's why I was capable of transforming from a sound sleeper to a world-champion track star with the ability to sprint down and up stairs at the speed of light. (Okay, maybe I wasn't *that* fast, but it sure did feel that way.)

Pretty cool, right? Well, I've got some good news, some not-so-good news, and then some really good news. The good news is that you don't need to keep yourself up at night worrying about whether you have what it takes to protect your child should an emergency arise. You do! Your always-on-guard amygdala will trigger your body to give you the mental clarity you need to think quickly and the physical energy to get into action. So you can cross that worry off your list. Whew!

Now for the not-so-good news. You know that marvelous, fast-acting, glorious amygdala of yours? Well, it doesn't differentiate between *real* danger and *imagined* danger. That means whether you actually need to protect yourself and your kids or you're simply worrying about things that might happen (you know, all of those what-ifs that keep you up at night), the amygdala interprets your stress-filled thoughts as a present and real threat and sounds the alarm. It doesn't recognize that you're merely imagining worst-case scenarios and contemplating what *might* go wrong. As you continue to worry, your brain signals the HPA axis to remain activated, and as a result, the stress-response hormones, which were designed to protect you in the event of a real emergency, can end up impairing your health.

> Your mind is falling for imagined danger like it's a "designer" purse sold on a hook at a flea market.

For example, persistent adrenaline surges can damage blood vessels and arteries, increase blood pressure, and raise the risk of heart attack and stroke. Elevated cortisol levels can contribute to weight gain and a buildup of fatty tissue; these levels increase appetite and increase storage of unused nutrients as fat.

But don't worry, Mama Bear. The really good news comes next: the entire CALM process has been designed to help you put the brakes on the stress response through mind, body, and spirit practices—and you're learning this process right now. Way to go!

Before we get into the details, here's a quick recap: Your brain doesn't differentiate between *real* danger and *imagined* danger.

Your mind is falling for imagined danger like it's a "designer" purse sold on a hook at a flea market.

It's not real! You'd never spend $11 on a polyester "Chanel" fanny pack. Okay, fine. You wouldn't buy it twice.

Ask Yourself: Am I in Physical Danger?

Suppose someone makes a negative comment about your parenting, and now you're worried about whether you're a "good mom." To help you stop buying into imagined danger and put the brakes on the stress response, try this assumption-busting question: "Am I in physical danger?" That gets a nope. (And you'll learn how to squash self-doubt in Chapter 8.)

What if you're going through separation or divorce, and you're worried about the kids' happiness and your financial stability? Are you in physical danger? No, Mama. It might feel that way, but in this moment you're safe, and more strategies to help you stop worrying—even in this instance—are coming in this book. So keep reading.

Let's try another scenario that's incredibly triggering for moms around the globe: mess and clutter.

Imagine you're sitting in your family room, and it's a mess. There are clothes to sort, paperwork to organize, and a seemingly endless array of toys to put away. (BTW, if you're one of those super-organized moms and you're thinking, *My house would never look like that!* then just for the sake of this exercise, try pretending your house is cluttered and messy right now—hmmm, is your heart racing yet?) All of this mess starts to trigger you. You wonder, *Where do I even start? If I was a good mom, the house wouldn't look like this. All I do is clean up messes and tend to everyone else's needs.*

This kind of stress—the environmental stress of mess—as well as psychological stress such as chronic worry about money, family difficulties, your children's happiness, and so on can set off the stress response. You'll know the stress response has been triggered when your heart starts to pound, your blood pressure goes up, and you begin to breathe faster as the surge of hormones floods your body.

Take a deep breath and ask yourself, "Am I in physical danger?"

In this scenario, are you in physical danger? Hint: The answer is no. Well, not unless those piles of toys are so high that they are about to avalanche down and suffocate you. And even though I do my best to avoid using all-or-nothing words like "always" and "never," I'm fairly certain that suffocating under an avalanche of dolls, Lego blocks, and video games is never going to happen to you. Even so, constant worry about the state of your house—or anything else for that matter—keeps the fight-flight-freeze mechanism in a chronic state of activation, and as mentioned earlier, that state impairs your health.

So consciously acknowledging you're not in physical danger will help put the brakes on the stress response. What if you're in a situation and you're not sure how to answer the question? Let's say you're in an abusive relationship, and the answer to the question is "I'm not in physical danger in this very moment, but I might be in the next moment." This is when you implement A, the second step in the CALM process: Act to Control the Controllable. Take the action of reaching out to the appropriate sources or organizations for help to get yourself to safety. Perhaps you need to reach out right now and call a helpline or shelter in your area. In cases like this, use your worry as a positive force and take action. I'll discuss how to do that in more depth in Part 2.

However, the majority of the time, your answer to the question "Am I in physical danger?" will be a resounding "No." If you were actually in physical danger (or in potential physical danger—as in the case of, let's say, the alarm in your house being triggered, meaning there might be an intruder inside), you'd likely already be taking action to protect yourself. Your stress response would guarantee it.

When you have consciously acknowledged that you're not in physical danger, take a few deep, calming breaths. Declare to yourself, "I am safe. I am not in physical danger." Then continue to take deep, calming breaths and bring your attention to the present moment. One way to do so is to focus on your five senses: sight, sound, smell, taste, and touch.

Here's one exercise you can try right now: Wiggle your toes. What do they feel like? Are they warm? Are you wearing soft socks or slippers? What can you hear right now? Maybe a bird chirping, a clock ticking, or car engines humming? Put a mint in your mouth. What does it taste like? Is it cool? How does it feel on your tongue? Is it smooth?

If you're feeling the stress response while trying to go to sleep, bring your attention to the present by thinking of an item in your room that starts with the letter "A," and then make your way through the alphabet. Armchair, blanket, cup, duvet, earrings, fan. You get the picture.

That's how I calmed myself down after the dogs and I ran upstairs to protect my children from the intruder. Once I realized that all was well and there was no real danger, I took a few deep breaths, gave each of my dogs a snuggle, put them back in the basement, and settled into my bed. Then, starting with the letter "A," I made my way through the alphabet, mentally listing items in my room that began with each letter. I fell asleep while trying to come up with something that begins with the letter "J."

The bottom line is that your brain doesn't know the difference between when you're *actually* in danger or when you're just imagining potential danger. When you conjure up frightening scenarios in your mind, your brain sets off the fight-flight-freeze response to keep you safe. This automatic response to stress is fabulous if you actually have to protect yourself from danger. However, if the only threat is your own thinking, it can really take a toll on your physical health. Do your mind and body a favor by consciously redirecting your thoughts to the present moment and acknowledging that you're not in physical danger.

Take a Break—Time for a Little Pun

Hey, Mama Bear, all of that stress-response talk was kind of heavy. So let's lighten things up and have a little "pun." Here are some riddles you can ask the kids:

Q: What does a brain do to greet a friend?

A: *It gives a brain wave.*

Q: Why didn't the brain take a shower?

A: *It didn't want to be brainwashed.*

Q: Where did the brain study at school?

A: *On the "Hippo Campus."*

Q: Why did the brain put on lipstick and mascara?

A: *It needed to make up its mind.*

Q: What is located in the middle of the brain?

A: *The letter A.*

Q: With which side of the brain is it better to write?

A: *Neither. It's better to use a pen.*

Riddle-culous Author Names and the Books They Haven't Written: Can You Solve the Puns?

The Stress Response by Amy G. Dala

Revved Up and Raring to Go by Cort T. Sol

Adrenal Fatigue by Y. R. U. Worried

CHAPTER 2

Differentiate between Fact and Opinion

Put Your Thoughts to the Test of Three

When my daughter Brianna was in third grade, she was given a homework assignment on facts and opinions. Her task was to read through about twenty statements and determine which of the statements were facts and which ones were opinions. Here are four of the statements, along with Brianna's answers:

¤ Some families have dogs as pets. *Fact.*

¤ Dogs are better pets than cats. *Opinion.*
¤ Apples grow on trees. *Fact.*
¤ A banana tastes disgusting. *Fact.*

In reviewing her answers, I noticed that Brianna had made a mistake with the last answer. I said, "Brianna, you said it's a fact that a banana tastes disgusting, but I ate one for breakfast today. So is it a fact or an opinion?" She replied, "It's a fact that you ate a disgusting banana for breakfast today!"

In my first book, I described this conversation with my daughter as an example of how important it is for us to challenge limiting beliefs. That morning, while reviewing the assignment with my daughter, I had a lightbulb moment. I had the realization that some of the beliefs we hang on to—even those that do more harm than good—are actually opinions, yet we live our lives as though they're facts.

We need to stop blindly mistaking opinion for fact. Too many of us carry around the pain of past criticisms, rejections, and putdowns because we have confused the two. Because of that, too many people have given up on their hopes and dreams.

Ask Yourself: Is It True? Is It Fact? Is It Helpful?

Whenever you hear or choose to hold a belief that limits you, challenge it. Ask yourself, "Is the belief I'm hearing or holding a fact or an opinion?" More often than not, you'll discover it's just an opinion. And you simply don't have to let negative opinions become your reality.

There's another equally important application of this question. In addition to using this question to challenge limiting beliefs, you can also use it to challenge your assumptions. What exactly is an assumption? An assumption is something you accept as true (or as certain to happen) without proof. Did you catch that? You accept it *without proof.*

Would you expect to be approved for a mortgage without proof of income? Would you expect your teenager to be given a driver's license without any proof they can drive? Would you expect to be able to board a commercial airplane or enter a foreign country without any proof of identification?

It's time to stop granting negative assumptions an all-access pass to your mind. When you're making assumptions that are causing you to worry, check in with your thinking. What proof do you have that what you're assuming is correct? Put your thoughts to the test of three. Ask yourself:

- **"Is it true?"**
- **"Is it fact?"**
- **"Is it helpful?"**

When I was a teenager, I wasn't equipped with these three questions. If I had known to challenge my assumptions, it certainly would have eased my anguish the day my boss came running out of the gas station, yelling, "Denise, go home!"

I was seventeen years old and pumping gas at a part-time job. A customer had pulled up in a beautiful red sports car. While his car was filling up with gas, I checked the oil and cleaned the windshield. Then I took the man's money and went inside to get his change. I handed it to him, flashed him a big smile, and said, "Have a great weekend!"

With that, he drove off—taking the entire gas pump with him! I had forgotten to take the nozzle out of his car. The entire apparatus came crashing down, and there was glass everywhere. That's precisely when my boss came out and yelled at me to go home.

I left and wandered around the streets of Toronto for hours, beating myself up and worrying. *Oh no*, I thought. *I've been fired! How could I have done something so stupid? I can't go home. I'm so embarrassed. How am I going to tell my friends and family that I've lost my first job?*

Eventually, I did go home, and later that night, my boss called. He said, "Denise, you're not fired. I was just really mad, so I sent you home because I didn't want to say something I would regret."

What can you take away from my experience? If you—or your child—worry about making mistakes, just remember, I practically ruined an entire gas station and didn't lose my job! Instead, I had scared myself with incorrect negative assumptions. Not only were they incorrect, but the outcome was far more positive than I could have imagined. In fact, when my boss told me over the phone that I wasn't fired, I replied, "I can't go back there. I'm too embarrassed!"

"But you're such a good worker," he said.

To convince me to come back to work at his gas station—which hours ago I had practically *destroyed*—he gave me a fifty-cent raise! Fortunately, I accepted the raise and resumed my job at the gas station for the rest of the summer. Yes, the outcome of our mistakes is often not as bad as we imagine it will be.

You can learn to deal with the facts instead of the what-ifs and the worst-case scenarios. When your thoughts have you all knotted up inside, put your assumptions to the test. Ask yourself, "What assumptions am I making? Are they based on facts? What proof do I have that what I'm thinking is true? Is what I'm thinking helpful?" If I'd known how to test my thinking back then, I could have challenged my assumption and ended my worry in a hurry. It might have looked something like this:

Assumption: I've been fired, and everyone is going to judge me for my mistake.

- **Is it true?** Well, it sure feels true. (But here's a hint for you: Not every thought you think is true, and just because something feels true doesn't make it true. You'll learn more about that in Part 4.)

- **Is it fact?** Nope. The fact is that my boss said, "Go home." He didn't say, "You're fired." (Is what you're assuming based on facts? If not, take the action of getting all the details. Your best line of defense against worry-inducing assumptions is to make sure you're dealing with the facts.)

¤ **Is it helpful?** Definitely not. I'm wandering around the streets of Toronto, too embarrassed to go home. Not helpful. (Are the things you're assuming helpful, or are you just frightening yourself with worst-case-scenario thinking?)

Check in with your thoughts. What have you been worrying about lately? Is some of the anxiety you're feeling coming from negative assumptions? If so, challenge your assumptions. Test your thoughts. Ask yourself: "Is the assumption I'm making true? Is it fact? Is it helpful?"

Take a Break—Fact or Opinion?

Your turn, Mama Bear. Brianna finished her homework assignment on facts and opinions, and it's time for you to complete yours. First, read the following scenario. Then review the list of statements. Indicate which ones are facts and which ones are opinions by circling the appropriate word.

Scenario: You're standing in the produce section of a grocery store with your child (if you have more than one child, choose one to imagine). You see a woman look over at you and your child. The woman smirks. She then leans over to the man beside her and says something you can't hear. They laugh. She looks your way again for a moment and puts some bananas into her cart, and then they turn and walk away.

¤ The woman said something about you or your child.
Fact or Opinion?
¤ You were in the produce section of the grocery store.

Fact or Opinion?
- ¤ The man and woman were laughing at you.
  Fact or Opinion?
- ¤ The woman looked over at you and your child.
  Fact or Opinion?
- ¤ The woman bought bananas.
  Fact or Opinion?
- ¤ A banana tastes disgusting.
  Fact or Opinion?

Results: Only one of these statements is a fact. Did you spot it? The only fact is that you were in the produce section of the grocery store. "Wait a minute!" you say. "The woman bought bananas. I saw her put bananas into her cart." Yes, she did put them into her cart. I'd also agree that it's highly likely that she took those bananas to the checkout counter and paid for them. However, we can't say it's a fact that she bought them unless we saw her do it. All we know for sure is the woman put bananas into her cart.

"Well, it's a fact that the woman looked over at me and my child. I saw her look at us." Is that a fact? Without asking her, can you be sure she wasn't actually looking at something else? Could she have been reading the sign over your head?

The point of this exercise is to become crystal clear on the difference between fact and opinion. It happens far too often that our inner peace, happiness, and joy are replaced with upset, worry, and fear, all because we mistook opinion for fact.

Your Feelings Come from Your Thoughts

Now, what I'm going to say next is very important in helping you to challenge your assumptions. As real as your assumptions *feel*, they are not always telling you the truth! Just because something *feels* true doesn't make it true.

For instance, suppose that in the "Take a Break" scenario earlier, the woman actually did look over at you and your child and then said something about you to the man beside her. If you couldn't hear what she said about you, how does that make you feel?

- ¤ If you think she judged you and said something unfavorable about you, you might feel bad about yourself or angry about the judgment.
- ¤ If you think she looked in your direction for a moment and said something that had nothing to do with you, you might feel indifferent.
- ¤ If you think she looked in your direction and said something positive about you, you might feel good about yourself.

How you feel comes from what you think. It comes from the story you tell yourself about what happened and the meaning and weight you give to it. It comes from the way you appraise the situation.

> As real as your assumptions *feel*, they are not always telling you the truth! Just because something *feels* true doesn't make it true.

How you appraise situations is largely dictated by your past experiences. If something is significant enough or happens often enough, your brain creates a neural pathway to help you interpret and respond to similar situations as quickly and efficiently as possible. As an example, imagine a dog bit you when you were a child. Now imagine you're an adult strolling down the street with your child and someone walking a dog is coming toward you. Based on experience, you might feel panicky, afraid, or anxious; you might even cross the street. On the other hand, someone who didn't have your experience of being bitten might not even notice the dog.

Another factor that influences how you appraise situations is those who surrounded you when you were growing up. Parents, teachers, coaches, and media figures have had an enormous impact on your belief system. They projected their thoughts and beliefs onto you, and it affected you, impacting the way you think.

Each of us have had experiences that shaped us in our formative years, and the beliefs and perceptions formed as a result can affect every area of our lives. Sometimes those experiences we had growing up were very positive. If your experiences in the past were mostly positive—you received lots of love while growing up, were valued and respected, and received constructive criticism as well as appropriate praise and encouragement—they would have likely led to a positive, realistic view of yourself.

On the other hand, if you had negative childhood experiences— such as being ignored, criticized, ridiculed, teased, or picked on regularly or being surrounded by unrealistically demanding parents or teachers—you would likely have developed a negative view of yourself, a lack of self-confidence, feelings of inferiority, and a great deal of self-doubt. Believe it or not, those past experiences can have a lot of staying power; they can continue to shape what you believe to be true about yourself as an adult.

How can this play out in our adult lives? These experiences can become problematic because they have created neural pathways that are more likely to lead to negative meanings, appraisals, and interpretations, which in turn can affect our emotions—and our emotions affect our actions. You'll learn more about this more in Part 4, "Master Your Mind," but for now, think of these neural pathways like the gutters on a bowling alley. When the bowling ball falls into the gutter, there's only one path the ball will be taking all the way down the lane. Similarly, when we latch onto a single interpretation, it's like we are deepening and strengthening that gutter, making it very difficult for the bowling ball to take any other path down the lane. This neural pathway becomes so powerful that it begins to eliminate other, more positive, interpretations and appraisals.

There is good news though: You're at a point in your life where you can make changes. You get to be the trainer of your mind. You can do so here and now by using the steps you're learning in this book. Diligently differentiating between fact and opinion will go a long way toward helping you make more accurate appraisals of situations you encounter, let go of worry-induced assumptions, and feel calmer.

CHAPTER 3

HALT Your Worries

Four Culprits behind Your Negative Assumptions

I stopped at the stop sign, and I stayed there. There wasn't a single car in sight. Yet I remained stopped at the intersection—waiting. The kids sat contentedly in their car seats in the back of the vehicle. My husband, whom I'd just picked up from the train station after his business trip, sat beside me in the passenger's seat. I'd been home alone with our six-week-old infant and two-year-old daughter for two nights. I hadn't had much sleep, and I was running on fumes.

As I continued to wait, my husband, confused, looked back and forth across the empty intersection. He waited a few more moments, then said, "Um, you can go now?"

I was so tired that I was waiting for the stop sign to turn into a go signal!

Motherhood comes with many awesome benefits (such as the superior mom strength that makes it possible to wrestle a pair of scissors out of the hands of a toddler who somehow has the grip strength of Dwayne "The Rock" Johnson). However, part of the motherhood package is also late—or sleepless—nights and early mornings. Lack of sleep can have real consequences. It's important to recognize that when you're feeling tired, you're more likely to make negative assumptions—the kind that cause you to worry. In fact, you're more likely to make those worry-inducing assumptions anytime you're feeling any of the following:

- Hungry
- Angry
- Lonely
- Tired

For many years, twelve-step programs have used the acronym HALT because they understand we're most likely to fall into behaviors from which we are trying to free ourselves when we are hungry, angry, lonely, or tired. The same goes for worry; when any one of these four are present, we are more likely to make incorrect assumptions that can cause worry.

For that reason, when you're making negative assumptions, it's important to HALT and check whether you're experiencing any of these four symptoms. If one or more are present, recognize that they are likely causing your assumptions to take a downward turn. Then take care of your needs and HALT your worries using the following suggestions.

Ask Yourself: Am I Hungry?

When you're hungry, it's quite possible the assumptions you're making are off base. To help you regain your perspective, acknowledge that your hunger may be driving your negative assumptions. Then remedy your hunger by eating. It's wise to choose something healthy to eat when you're feeling worried or stressed. Otherwise, you might end up feeling guilty about what you've just eaten, which may cause your worry to grow.

The key is to eat before your assumptions, thoughts, and emotions have a chance to escalate. One way to keep hunger at bay throughout the day is to include protein in every meal. Protein—meat, chicken, fish, eggs, legumes, dairy products, nuts, and seeds—can help prevent you from getting hungry and give you energy, clarity, and focus to take on the day. Have protein for breakfast? Yes and yum! Plain, nonfat Greek yogurt has twenty grams of protein in just seven ounces. Two large eggs contain thirteen grams of protein. Two tablespoons of peanut butter will give you eight grams of protein. There are so many delicious protein-rich food choices available to help you stay satiated throughout the day and prevent you from making hunger-induced assumptions.

Perhaps if they'd just tried a handful of almonds, Romeo's and Juliet's parents could have been catalysts to a happier ending.

One step past hunger is "hanger." Have you ever been hangry? You know what I'm talking about—it's that irritable or angry feeling some people get when they're hungry. As well as being one of the leading causes of negative assumptions, hunger is also a major contributor to a grumpy mood. Have you ever said "Mmmmm" to yourself when you finally got a chance to eat? Perhaps that's your mouth signaling to your good mood that it's safe to return!

Ask Yourself: Am I Angry?

Anger is a powerful emotion. It can cause you to make rash decisions and ramp up the speed of negative thinking. We all feel angry or impatient from time to time, and it's okay for you to feel the way you do. In Chapter 19, "Regulate Your Emotions," you'll learn a system to regain your inner peace before reacting out of anger—or any other upset emotion, for that matter. There are many effective strategies ahead in this book!

In the meantime, try this method to calm anger-induced assumptions. First, if you're feeling angry, acknowledge that this powerful emotion may be the culprit behind your worst-case-scenario thinking. Next,

When you use anger to identify your unmet needs and then take care of those needs, anger becomes a gift of sorts.

halt and take deep, calming breaths. Anger ramps up your thinking, and taking deep, calming breaths helps to slow it down. With practice, you'll become such a chill mom that you'll watch action movies and say to your partner, "If the Hulk would just take some deep breaths, he wouldn't feel the need to throw that helicopter at that building." (To which your adoring partner will murmur, "Babe, I'm trying to watch the movie.")

After taking a few calming breaths, write your feelings down. Mind you, don't write them down in an email and hit send! Sending an email or leaving a message in anger is definitely not a good idea—even if it feels like it will give you some release in the moment. It will just end up causing more stress for you down the road. A better way to get the release you crave is to vent your feelings onto paper, then tear it up and toss it out!

In addition to venting your feelings down on paper, recognize anger as a potential unmet need. How are you hurting? In which areas do you need more help and support? Do you need to ask your partner or kids to pitch in more around the house?

When you use anger to identify your unmet needs and then take care of those needs, anger becomes a gift of sorts. You'll learn more about that when we get to Chapter 9, which talks about self-care. Until then, Mama Bear, when you're feeling angry, be aware that this feeling may be the culprit behind your negative assumptions.

Ask Yourself: Am I Lonely?

Motherhood can feel lonely at times. You may feel anxious or depressed, which can cause you to withdraw and avoid spending time with others. When you become a mom, your interests change. On top of that, it can be challenging to find time to socialize. Have you ever tried scheduling a kid-free meeting with another overwhelmed mom? It's like you're negotiating to release hostages: "Meet me outside the library on the Thursday after Thanksgiving, and I'll bring you a nonfat cappuccino. We'll speak for eight uninterrupted minutes. I could not secure the helicopter you requested, but an Uber will be supplied."

If you're feeling lonely, acknowledge that it could be the real reason behind your what-if thinking and negative assumptions. Sometimes just knowing the reason for our thinking can help to calm a worried mind.

Recognize your feelings of loneliness as an unmet need. Human beings need connection. We're not meant to be alone. Yes, it can be tricky to make time for those important human connections. However, reaching out to another doesn't have to be elaborate. Is there a friend you've been meaning to text, even if just for a short chat? Who could you connect with or check in on today?

Are you at a stage in parenting during which you have a little more time on your hands? Try out new hobbies and interests. Do you feel like you have a bee in your bonnet? Join an urban beekeeping collective, honey! Do you have the feeling you're walking on eggshells? A speed-walking group might be just your crowd. What about an upholstery class? If mom life has got you on the edge of your seat, it might as well be on a really nice chair!

It's healthy to maintain your identity in motherhood. Do what you can to build connection with others. Nurture your close friendships and foster new ones.

Ask Yourself: Am I Tired?

Do you ever reflect back on the days before you had kids, days when you thought you were tired and busy? I sure do. I didn't realize how much sleep and free time I'd actually had before my babies were born! I wouldn't change it for the world, and I'm guessing you feel the same. Being a mom is super rewarding. Hearing your child laugh, getting hugs, and feeling the incredible amount of love bursting in your heart makes those sleepless nights and busy days all worth it.

But on those days when you're feeling a little fatigued—or completely exhausted—it's important to be aware that feeling tired can trigger negative assumptions. Here are some remedies to help you combat fatigue.

Stay Hydrated

You thought the first thing I was going to tell you was to sleep more, didn't you? Getting good-quality sleep does play a significant role in vitality and emotional well-being, but there are stages in a mom's life where getting adequate sleep isn't an option: the newborn stage, the my-toddler-keeps-getting-out-of-bed-every-night stage, the my-child-is-sick stage, the my-teenager-is-out-past-curfew stage. You get the picture.

Whichever stage you're in won't last forever, and you will survive it! But during the times you're not getting enough sleep, there's still something you can do: stay hydrated. Being dehydrated can cause you to feel even more tired, and feeling tired can lead to negative assumptions, so make sure you're drinking enough water. In addition to relieving fatigue, drinking water also increases energy and flushes out toxins. When you're feeling tired, ask yourself, "Have I met my water goal today?"

Get Adequate Sleep

If you're at a phase of parenting in which you're able to get sleep, do what you can to prioritize sleep. In his book *Keep Sharp: Build a Better Brain at Any Age,* Dr. Sanjay Gupta writes, "Chronic inadequate sleep puts people at a higher risk for dementia, depression and mood disorders, learning and memory problems, heart disease, high blood pressure, weight gain and obesity, diabetes, fall-related injuries, and cancer. It can even trigger biases in behavior, causing you to focus on negative information when making decisions."[3]

Focusing on negative information is certainly one of the ways in which worry grows. That's why this section of the HALT strategy is the longest. Here are some ideas to help you get an adequate night's slumber:

Reset your body clock. When your body clock is feeling more like a cuckoo clock, it's time for a reset! Go to bed and wake up at the same time every day. This really works. Your body clock will settle into a pattern, and over time, you'll find you wake up just before the alarm goes off. I know from personal experience that it's undeniably more refreshing to wake up naturally instead of to the sound of the alarm.

Write your worries down. Sometimes we play a worry over and over again in our minds because we are worried we'll forget what we're worried about! If worry is keeping you up at night, keep a pen and paper beside the bed. If a worry comes up when you're trying to sleep, write it down. This mental dumping process clears the worry from your mind so you can sleep. By writing your worry down, you won't forget it, and you can take action on it—using the strategies you're learning in this book—at a time when you aren't trying to sleep. Avoid writing your worries in your cell phone; the lights on an electronic device can affect your sleep cycles and wakefulness, plus you don't want to be tempted to check any text messages that might have come in while you've been tossing and turning.

Try magnesium. If you're having trouble falling asleep or staying asleep, it's a good idea to talk with your health care provider or naturopathic doctor. There may be holistic treatments that can help you overcome this hurdle and get the sleep you require.

Magnesium can be extremely effective in getting a good night's sleep. (Here's a note of caution, though: make sure to check in with your health care provider before taking magnesium if you're pregnant, nursing, or on medications.)

Consider chamomile tea. Chamomile is known for its soothing and sedative effects. This is a great tea to drink before bedtime! In addition to relaxing tense muscles, chamomile tea has been said to induce sleep. (Again, check in with your health care provider before drinking this natural-remedy tea if you're pregnant, nursing, or on medications.)

Using these strategies will help you do what you can to get a good night's sleep. Getting solid zzz's each night can calm a worried mind.

The next time your assumptions are causing you to worry, HALT. Ask yourself, "Am I hungry, angry, lonely, or tired?" If you're experiencing even one of those symptoms, recognize it may be the reason behind your unpleasant conclusions and follow the suggestions outlined. HALT negative assumptions before they erode your inner peace.

Take a Break—Now for a Little Play . . .

A Little Screenplay, That Is!

INT. KITCHEN—NIGHT

MOM and TEENAGER are sitting at a kitchen table. MOM places a bowl of steamed veggies and a plate of baked chicken breasts on the table.

TEENAGER has a weird look on his face.

TEENAGER

(*grunts*) New recipe?

MOM

Yes, I've decided we're going to eat better. The protein will help me stop getting hangry during the day, which means I can think better and make fewer hunger-based negative assumptions.

TEENAGER

Huh?

MOM

Eating this way will help us to live long and healthy lives.

TEENAGER

Will we actually live longer eating this way, or will it just feel longer?

CHAPTER 4

Rate the Probability

Probability versus Possibility

The time had come to register our little one into kinder-garten. As a first step, I decided to visit the local public elementary school and meet the principal. While my husband and I were walking down the school's hallway, the bell rang, signaling the end of class. Instantly, children filed out of their classrooms and filled the corridor.

I turned to my husband and said, "Look at all of these kids in the hall. There isn't any supervision. I could just take any one of them and leave." That idea worried me so much that we left the school and registered our daughter into a private school.

Nelson Mandela said, "May your choices reflect your hopes, not your fears." My fear drove me to do the opposite of Mandela's wise advice. I didn't make the decision based on the hopes of a better education for my child. I made it because, unlike the public school, the private school had a locked-door policy. You had to ring the doorbell to be let into the school, *and* you had to sign your child out of class before your little one could leave.

At that time, I was still a worrier, and I didn't yet know how to challenge my assumptions. As a result, I made a decision based on fear. If I'd had the information you're learning right now, I would have been able to calm my worry and make a decision based on what was best for our family—including what was best for us financially. Private school was expensive. Ouch!

Ask Yourself: On a Scale of 1 to 10, How Probable Is It That What I'm Worried about Will Happen?

If I knew then what I know now, I would have asked myself, "How probable is it that what I'm worried about will happen?" In other words, how likely is it that my child will be abducted from school?

My answer would have been: "The probability is very low."

You might be thinking, *But Denise, it could happen.* Yes, and I *could* win the lottery. But that doesn't change the fact that the probability of it happening is extremely low. In fact, can you guess how many children have been abducted from that school since it opened over thirty years ago? Exactly zero!

It's important to understand I'm not denying the fact that bad things can and do happen. Precautions are important. Part of taking precautions as a parent is to prepare and equip your kids.

When I was a little girl, one of the ways in which my mom prepared and equipped me was by instructing me to never talk to strangers. She would test me to find out if her advice had finally sunk in, asking, "Denise, if a stranger offered you candy, what would you do?" My response was always the same: "I'd take the candy and then run away really, really fast." She insisted I should just leave the candy and then run away from the stranger. I quipped that I could run so fast that not only would I be safe but I'd also have some free candy.

While it may not have appeared that way to my mom, I actually was absorbing her words. And I remembered them the day a stranger asked me to get into his car. I was eight years old at the time.

It was raining that day, and I was standing at the bottom of a long wooden staircase that led to the yard at the back of my school.

The stranger stopped his car next to me. "Are you going to school?" he called through his passenger-side window.

I answered, "Yes." Pointing to the top of the stairs, I continued, "This is my school."

"Get in the car and I'll drive you," he said.

"But it's just at the top of these stairs," I said. The staircase had been built as a shortcut. Without the stairs, students had to walk an extra twenty minutes or so, up the steep sidewalk and around the street corner to get to the front of the school.

"It's raining. Get in the car and I'll drive you," he repeated.

The situation didn't feel right, and I bolted up the stairs without another word. I didn't tell my mom or my teacher about my encounter with the stranger. I can't even remember whether I told one of my friends. All I remember is clearly knowing not to get into that man's car.

In my first book, *CALM: A Proven Four-Step Process Designed Specifically for Women Who Worry,* I wrote in the "Transform Fears into Action" section about a similar experience that happened to me when I was fourteen. You can read about that story there, but the point is that *twice* in my life I had to run from "stranger danger." This history is likely why I was worried about my own child being abducted from school. As I noted earlier, many of our fears are based on past experiences, and I'll have more on that coming up.

Right now, go ahead and think about the assumptions you're making that are driving your present concerns. What are you worrying will occur? Rate the probability of it actually happening on a scale of 1 to 10. 1 = least likely to happen, and 10 = most likely to happen.

- ¤ **Did you rate your worry a 5 or less?** This low rating on the scale of probability is a fair indication that what you're worried about isn't going to happen. Acknowledging this low risk can sometimes be enough to help you reconnect with your inner peace.

- ¤ **Did you rate your worry a 9 or less?** Keep calm, Mama Bear. There's still a good chance that what you're worried about isn't going to occur. In fact, have you ever noticed that many of the things you've agonized over in the past didn't end up happening?

- ¤ **Did you rate your worry a 10?** This rating indicates that you feel what you're worried about is extremely likely to happen. Take a deep breath, because there's hope! The next three steps in the CALM process will help you let go of worry—even those worries with a 10 rating—by taking action to control the things you can and letting go of the things beyond your control.

A Case Study: How Justine Got Calm

A student of my CALM Online training course,[4] Justine, used this strategy of rating the probability to help her move out of panic mode. At the beginning of the COVID-19 pandemic in 2020, she received an email from her son's school about the coronavirus.

She worried, thinking, "Why am I getting this letter? Does it mean there's coronavirus at my child's school? Is it possible he has it?"

Often when we are worried, we ask ourselves, "Is it possible that what I'm worried about will happen?" The answer is yes—of course it's possible. All things are possible. Anything can happen. That's why, when we think about the unlimited possibilities of what might go wrong in any given situation, an enormous amount of anxiety can set in. So change it around. Instead of asking, "Is it possible?" ask, "Is it probable?" On the scale of 1 to 10, how *likely* is it that what you're worrying about is going to happen?

To help rate the probability, Justine made sure she was dealing with facts. First, she called another parent whose little one attended a different school and asked if she had received a similar email. Her friend had indeed received one. This information helped Justine to understand that the email wasn't sent to her specifically because there was an outbreak at her son's school (which was one of the assumptions creating so much mental anguish). The email was an information notice sent to all parents whose children attended schools in the region (fact).

Next, Justine armed herself with the knowledge that there were less than forty cases of coronavirus in all of Canada at that time. With that fact, she rated the probability of her child contracting the illness—at that exact moment—as very low on the scale of probability, and it calmed her mind. It's these subtle shifts in thinking that can transform worry into inner peace.

Doing this is not to dismiss the risk. As mentioned earlier, precautions are important. Justine followed the recommended safety precautions (such as teaching her little one about proper handwashing), but when she received the email from the school, and in the moment her panic started to set in, she was able to regain her inner peace by asking herself, "Is it *probable* my son will come home with coronavirus today when there are only forty cases in all of Canada and none in our region?" Her answer was "It's not probable."

This assumption-busting process is designed to help you avoid giving in to panic, an important skill when crisis hits. In an interview on CTV's news program W5 in March 2020, Dr. Bruce Aylward (a renowned epidemiologist from the World Health Organization in Geneva, Switzerland) said:

> *We are watching an outbreak evolve, so people should be concerned, they should be informed, they should be doing the right things and managing it; but panicking is definitely not going to help.*

When "what-if" thoughts take over your thinking, remember to rate on a scale of 1 to 10 the probability of what you're worrying about actually happening.

You panic when you're on a sinking boat in the middle of the ocean with no lifeboat and you can't swim. This isn't that situation.

We know how to manage it, and there's so much that can be done. So be concerned, be prepared, but panicking is not going to help you in this situation, and you don't need to. There's so much you can do at an individual level to protect yourself.[5]

There it is: Be prepared. But do not panic.

You weren't meant to live your life in fear. What you can do instead is challenge your assumptions so you can stop worrying about things that are not likely to happen (what you're learning right now), take action to control the controllable (coming up in Part 2), and let go of the uncontrollable (coming up in Part 3).

When "what-if" thoughts take over your thinking, remember to rate on a scale of 1 to 10 the probability of what you're worrying about actually happening. In addition, instead of asking, "Is it possible that what I'm worried about will happen?" ask, "Is it probable that what I'm worried about will happen?" That subtle shift in thinking can prevent you from going into panic mode and connect you with a sense of calm.

Take a Break—Fill In the Love

In this chapter, you've learned how to challenge your assumptions by rating the probability of your worries. You also heard how my mom's advice when I was a child equipped and prepared me to stay safe when she wasn't with me. You are already working to equip and prepare your children too. Trust that they'll hear your voice when it's time for them to make big decisions—that will help you to retain your inner peace.

For that reason, let's play a game called "Fill In the Love." If your child is old enough, or you have a partner willing to play, have your child or partner answer the following questions. Otherwise, you can answer them yourself.

1. What is something you worry about regarding your child?
2. What is one piece of advice you tell them over and over again?
3. What is your child's (or children's) name(s)?

Using the answers to those three questions, fill in the blanks in the letter that follows (an excerpt from *Knock Knock: Letters to My Wonderful Mom Read Me When Box*[6]):

Dear Mom,

Look, I know you worry, about big things and little things, and [**Answer #1**]. But just know that I am always careful, and most of the time I hear your voice in my head anyway, saying something like, "[**Answer #2**]." So even when you're not with me, you're with me! (And it's gonna be okay.)

Love, [**Answer #3**].

Mama Bear, my daughter Lindsay filled in the blanks in the letter for me. She's married now with two children of her own! Here's the letter from my kiddo:

Dear Mom,

Look, I know you worry, about *me eating enough*, and *Bri and me being happy*. But just know that I am always careful, and most of the time I hear your voice in my head anyway, saying something like, *"You really need to read my book." (LOL—I love you!)* So even when you're not with me, you're with me! (And it's gonna be okay.) *And me and Bri are going to be okay!*

Love, *Linds*

Reading that letter really does give me comfort. Fill in your letter too as a reminder from your child—or from yourself—that it really is going to be okay!

CHAPTER 5

End What-If Thinking

The Three Cures

Immediately after I told my mom I was expecting, she declared, "Now you'll never have a worry-free day the rest of your life."

I was twenty-two years old, and I thought my mom was wrong. *Of course I'm worried right now. I'm pregnant. What if the baby isn't moving enough? What if there's something wrong? What if something bad happens during labor? It's a scary time. But when the baby is born, and I can see that he or she is healthy, then I won't worry anymore.*

Finally, that day arrived—or so I thought. My original due date had already come and gone. (Ugh!) I was seven days overdue and heading to the hospital to be induced. The contractions went on through the entire night. In the morning, I was informed the induction was unsuccessful, and they sent me home! I was not a happy camper.

Six days later, and guess what? No baby yet. As I sat on the examination table with a paper sheet draped over my legs, my gynecologist said, "We're going to induce you again tomorrow."

"Please don't. It didn't work last time," I begged.

"I promise you that this time you won't leave the hospital until you have that baby," my doctor assured me.

At this point, I was fifty-four pounds heavier than I had been nine and a half months earlier, and I wanted this baby out. So, with the doctor's promise that tomorrow would be the day, I agreed to get induced again.

After another long night and a seemingly endless day of contractions, the doctor came into my hospital room. "You're not dilating," he said. "We have to send you home."

Nooooooooooooooooooo! I felt miserable, and I worried: *What if this never ends?*

When I was seventeen days overdue, the gynecologist called me and said, "I need to see you in my office this afternoon." Immediately I thought, *What if something's wrong?*

I arrived at his office, and he told me, "I need to book you in for a cesarean section tomorrow. You can't keep that baby in there forever."

I was nervous about a cesarean but also relieved there was finally an end date. I could finally meet my baby. I could finally put an end to all of the what-if thinking!

That very same night, my contractions started—on their own. This baby was coming without being induced and without a cesarian. The next afternoon, eighteen days overdue, I gave birth to my healthy baby girl. Now all of the worries about my child would end, right?

Wrong. I didn't stop worrying. In fact, after my daughter was born, I worried even more about her: *What if she's not eating enough? What if that rash is something serious? What if I can't find a good babysitter when I go back to work? What if the kids at school bully her like they did me? What if she doesn't pass her exams? What if she gets hurt on that class trip?*

Does any of this sound familiar to you? What do you worry about when it comes to your child (or children)? Is it safety, health, happiness, nutrition, development, friendships, education, or future?

> Worrying does not prevent unwanted things from happening—but it does steal the joy of parenting from you.

Is it something else? Deep down, many moms feel that worry gives them some sort of superpower—an ability to stop certain things from happening to our kids if we just worry hard enough. Worrying does not prevent unwanted things from happening—but it does steal the joy of parenting from you.

My constant worry kept me from enjoying the parenting experience in those early years. Until, that is, I learned a way to put an end to what-if thinking. It worked for me, and it will work for you too. Here are three cures for what-if thinking: two questions plus an affirmation. Before you lose any more sleep or waste any more time and energy on "what-if" thoughts, try implementing these three cures.

Ask Yourself: What Is?

Instead of "What if?" ask, "What is?" The purpose of this question is to bring your attention back to the present moment. Usually when we are worried, we are thinking about things that could go wrong in the future. You're not yet in the future. You're no longer in the past. You're right here, right now.

What is happening right here and right now? Right here and right now, you're safe. Right here and right now, you have the ability to take action to control the controllable and let go of the uncontrollable—which are the next two steps coming up for you in the CALM process.

For instance, suppose you're worried about finding the right childcare provider before you go back to work. Stop the what-if game by asking yourself, "What is?" In the present moment, you're not yet back at work. You're with your child. Right now, you're both safe. Right now, you can research childcare providers, ask friends for referrals, make some calls, and conduct some interviews with potential candidates. In this very moment, you're okay. Take a few slow, deep breaths and bring your thoughts back to the present moment.

What is good right now? Sometimes we can be so focused on all the things that might go wrong that we can forget to pay attention to all the things that are right. What is going your way? What things are you thankful for today? What good things are possible? Focusing on what is good right now will help you to remain calm and retain your inner peace.

Ask Yourself: Will It Matter a Year from Now?

The purpose of this question is to restore your perspective. What if your mother-in-law is ticked off that you chose to spend Thanksgiving with your family this year? What if you have to call in sick for work to take care of your child? What if you let all the messages and texts you received this morning sit unanswered while you take time to enjoy your life or take action on a goal you've had on the back burner for a while? Okay. Will any of these things matter a year from now? It's not very likely. In fact, most of the things we worry about are not that serious in the grand scheme of things.

When you're feeling worried, use this question to help you look at the bigger picture. If your answer to the question is no, you'll feel more at peace. However, if your answer is yes, move on to the third cure.

Affirm to Yourself: I'm Capable of Handling It—and My Kids Are Too!

Mama Bear, think about everything you've handled up to this point in your life. Reflect for a moment on the unexpected situations you've faced and all of the things you've dealt with that were even more challenging than you'd anticipated—like *motherhood*, for instance. You've been able to manage everything that's already come your way. I'm not suggesting you managed all of life's challenges effortlessly or without shedding tears. I'm saying you made it through all of your past experiences, and here you are today reading this book. Bravo, Mama Bear!

A quote often attributed to Linda Wooten goes like this: "Being a mother is learning about strengths you didn't know you had and dealing with fears you didn't know existed." You're strong! You've handled all of the cards that life has dealt to you so far. Believe that you will be able to manage whatever lies ahead for you and your family too. Instead of worrying about tomorrow, begin declaring, "I'm capable of handling it—and my kids are too!"

Besides, have you ever noticed that most of what you worry about never happens? The big things that happen to us are usually things we didn't conjure up in our wildest imaginations. Have you had one of those unexpected twists in life? Were you surprised by just how well you handled it? I sure surprised myself as a teenager when I was suddenly thrust into a life-threatening situation.

I have a newspaper clipping I keep in my desk drawer with a photo of me and my friend above the headline "Thirteen-year-old pulled friend from frozen Lake Simcoe."

Yup, I fell through the ice when I was thirteen years old! I'd been out walking with two friends on the ice of Lake Simcoe. While my two friends were talking with each other, I wandered off by myself. The ice was slushy. Using my boots, I made piles of slush and then jumped on them to watch it splatter.

The last pile I made was nice and big. I knew this one was going to make a tremendous splash, and I jumped on it with all my might. This time, I felt the knees of my pants get wet. I thought, *Oh no! I've fallen on the ice, and now my pants are soaked.* Then I felt my hair whoosh up like it did when I would jump into a swimming pool. *Oh my gosh. I haven't fallen on the ice. I've fallen through it!*

But the most unexpected thing happened while I was under the ice: I didn't panic. Instead, I felt calm. Now I know it was the stress response doing its job. The fight-flight-freeze response had been activated, giving my mind the clarity it required to deal with this very real danger. As a result, my thinking became crystal clear: *Get your hands out of your pockets, take off your mittens and boots, and then kick your feet so you stay near the surface.*

Fortunately for me, one of my friends had noticed I was missing. She turned to our other friend and asked, "Where's Denise?" She scanned the ice and saw the hole. She ran to the hole, plunged her arm into the icy water, and fished around until she found my hair, grabbed it, and pulled me out until she could grab my arm. Then this brave thirteen-year-old friend of mine pulled me back up through the hole and saved my life.

One thing I learned from that experience is that when you're in a life-or-death situation, your survival instincts drive you into focusing on the present moment. While I was under the ice, I was no longer worried about whether I had done well on my last exam. I was no longer stressing about going back to school after the spring break. All of my mental energy was focused on that exact moment.

Being laser focused on the present gave me the clarity to take the actions that kept me near the hole in the ice. This made it possible for my friend to rescue me. On the other hand, if I had lost focus on the present and started worrying about the possibilities of what might happen, panic and fearful thoughts would have surely set in. If that had happened, my friend might not have been able to reach my hair and rescue me that afternoon.

What can you take from this story? After all, it's not very likely you'll fall through the ice. However, there will be challenges throughout your life when your response will have a significant impact on the outcome. It could be the breakdown of a marriage, a serious illness in the family, or financial difficulty. During such times, remember that what-if thinking sinks you and present-moment thinking pulls you through.

Get present by focusing on what is. Restore your perspective by asking whether it will matter a year from now. While you're at it, instead of thinking, "What if things don't turn out?" ask yourself, "What if they do?" How about using that incredible imagination of yours to picture things turning out exactly as you hope they will? Keep your hopes up. Believe in the possibilities. And believe in your ability to handle whatever the future brings. Affirm: "I am capable of handling it—and my kids are too!"

You really are capable. You're one strong Mama Bear!

CHAPTER 6

Rewrite the Story

How to Stop Scaring Yourself with Worst-Case Scenarios

"Your daughter is struggling with reading," Brianna's third-grade teacher told me. "She's not at the level she should be at this point, and I'm concerned."

Oh no! I thought. *My child is struggling. My child isn't reading at the level she should be. It's my fault. I haven't been reading with her at night. I've been working too much, and I've been too tired. I'm a bad mom. What about Brianna? What will become of her?*

Yup! I had taken the teacher's two sentences and made the worry-inducing assumptions that it was all my fault and that

Brianna's entire life was ruined. I'm not exaggerating. I really was worried that I had ruined her life. Sound familiar, Mama Bear? Have you ever taken a present situation and pictured a completely disastrous future outcome?

Worry is often generated by the scary stories we tell ourselves. The scary stories you tell yourself are created in your imagination, and they are seldom accurate. Did you catch that? Your worst-case scenarios are rarely correct! One of the traits of worriers is they tend to have fantastic imaginations. When you allow your imagination to be filled with negative assumptions, worry can consume you. However, when you choose to imagine the best-case scenario, worry loses its grip on you.

> Worry is often generated by the scary stories we tell ourselves.

So let's start using that incredible imagination of yours to your advantage. This next assumption-busting question will help you stop frightening yourself with scary stories and start using your imagination positively—by rewriting the story.

Ask Yourself: What Else Could It Be?

You can begin to rewrite the story by asking yourself, "What else could it be?" Obviously, to answer this question you're going to have to make more assumptions. But this time, make positive ones.

It's important to understand that asking "What else could it be?" is not meant to replace reality. Remember, your best line of defense for letting go of worry is to deal strictly with facts.

This question is meant to help you focus on a positive explanation in that time between the first inkling of worry and the relief of getting the facts. Doing so will help you maintain your peace of mind during that window of time.

Going back to my daughter's struggle with reading, my negative assumptions were these: *It's all my fault, and now her life is ruined.* But what else could it be? What could be some positive reasons that my daughter was struggling? Maybe she needed to have her vision and hearing checked. Maybe she needed to be tested for dyslexia to determine the best way for her to learn.

So we had her tested for dyslexia. The expert's conclusion was that my daughter wasn't dyslexic. Next, we had her hearing tested. The results indicated that Brianna's hearing was fine now; however, in the past she had experienced chronic ear infections, which would have made hearing difficult in those first years at school. Finally, we had her vision tested. Bingo! Brianna needed glasses. This sweet girl of mine was struggling with reading because she needed glasses and had had a difficult time hearing in those early years.

With her new glasses and her ear infections cleared up, we hired a tutor to help her get caught up. Not only did she catch up, she eventually graduated high school with honors. Then she went on to graduate from college—once again with honors. And I had worried that I had ruined her life. Oh, Mama Bear. Negative assumptions create unnecessary worry.

Here's another scenario: Your employer sends you a text message, saying, *I need to see you first thing tomorrow morning.*

Reading that text message will trigger your thoughts. Your thoughts will, in turn, trigger your emotions. For instance, if upon receiving that text message, your thoughts were positive or neutral, you will feel positive or neutral emotions. However, if your thoughts consisted of a list of possible negative reasons for why your boss wants to see you, they will trigger feelings of stress and worry.

At times, your emotions can be triggered so quickly and be so overpowering that you may have a difficult time recognizing how you ended up feeling the way you do. Try the following suggestions to help you organize your thoughts and restore your inner peace between that first inkling of worry and the relief of getting the facts:

1. **Identify the worry-trigger.** Ask yourself, "What did I see, hear, or read that triggered my current worry or fear?" Write down the event or situation that triggered your worried thoughts. You might write, *My boss sent me a text message saying she wants to meet tomorrow morning.*

2. **Identify your scary thoughts.** Ask yourself, "What is my scary story?" List any negative assumptions you're imagining about your current situation. Your story might sound like this: *What did I do wrong? What if I'm getting fired? If I get fired, what if I can't find another job with similar hours? What if my next employer doesn't give me the time I need to pick up my kids after school? What if I can't find a good person to look after my kids?* So now it's gone from a simple text from your boss about wanting to see you all the way to the giant fear of not being able to find someone to help with childcare. (See what I mean? People who tend to worry have incredible imaginations!) When you fill in the missing pieces of information with negative assumptions, what you're doing is frightening yourself with scary stories. It's time to stop scaring yourself.

3. **Start seeking out the facts.** Your best line of defense for letting go of worry is to deal strictly with facts. Ask yourself, "What actually happened or is happening?" and then find out what you don't know. In this scenario, you could take the action of responding with a text acknowledging you received your employer's message and asking if she could give you a heads up about the purpose of the meeting. However, you might not get an immediate response. If that's the case, calm your worry by trying to think of more positive explanations.

4. **Fill in the missing pieces with positive assumptions.** Ask yourself, "What else could it be?" List positive explanations to fill in the missing pieces. Maybe your employer wants to talk about a new project, or get a quick update

on your workload, or find out which days you plan on taking off next year so the company can plan accordingly. Maybe you did something worthy of recognition, and you're going to be acknowledged for your hard work.

Think that last one is far-fetched? It isn't. Recently, one of my friends was asked to meet with his employer regarding job performance. He was so stressed before the meeting that he couldn't sleep, and the day of the meeting, he sweated through his shirt! However, during the meeting, his boss gave him a glowing review and praised him for the good work he'd been doing. All of that stress just because of negative assumptions.

When assumptions are causing you to worry, and you don't yet have the facts, think of more positive explanations before your negative assumptions get the chance to build momentum. When you practice assuming the best on a regular basis, it will become a habit, and worry will lose its hold on you. Over time, you'll discover that the positive assumptions are correct more often than the negative ones.

However, what if your negative assumptions in your scary story had been right? Would it have been foolish to focus on the positives? That gets a nope! Worry doesn't change the outcome. And here's something else to consider: If you worry that the worst will happen, and then it does, you experience pain twice. If you believe in a favorable outcome, and the worst happens, you experience pain only once! Of course, if you believe in a favorable outcome, and the outcome is favorable, you don't experience any pain at all. Remind yourself, as we covered in the lesson "End What-If Thinking: The Three Cures," that whatever happens, you are capable of handling it!

I acknowledge that the scary stories and the positive stories are both still stories. Yet one induces fear, while the other induces calm and helps you to move forward. The next time your negative thinking is spiraling out of control, remember to seek out the facts. In the meantime, calm your worried mind by filling in the missing pieces with positive assumptions. Ask yourself, "What else could it be?" This slight change in your thought process will dramatically help you to decrease your worry and increase your peace of mind.

Well, Mama Bear, you're officially equipped to let go of worry in a hurry by challenging your assumptions. From now on, any-time worry is doing its best to make you feel stressed, use the six assumption-busting strategies you've just learned. (For a quick action list of these strategies, check out the Transformation Tracking Sheets in Part 5!)

Once you've challenged your assumptions, move to the second step in the CALM process and the second part of this book. Let's go there now!

PART 2

Act to Control the Controllable

When you feel worry brewing, instead of sitting there stewing, get up and start doing.

Did you know not all worry is bad? That's right. Some worry is actually good for you. Sometimes it's saying, "Hey, pay attention! There are some actions you need to take to protect your health, your wealth, yourself, your family, and your business."

Our babysitter was thrust into action the day she discovered my daughter's mouth was full of children's chewable pain-relief tablets. Yikes! My daughter Lindsay, a toddler at the time, had snuck into her babysitter's purse, opened the bottle of medicine, and popped the entire contents into her mouth. By the time the babysitter saw her, Lindsay was happily chomping away.

The babysitter ran over to Lindsay and, using her finger, took as much of the medicine out of my daughter's mouth as she could. Then she called the Poison Control Helpline.

"The toddler I'm looking after has just eaten children's pain-relief tablets," the panicky babysitter explained. "I don't know how many she swallowed. The bottle was nearly full!"

The helpline operator asked for the details of the medication and the size of the bottle. "It's okay," the operator assured her. "Even if she ate that entire bottle, this particular medication isn't strong enough to hurt a toddler. She is going to be just fine."

This story is a great example of how worry can serve as a prompt to take action and how the second step in the CALM process comes into play: A for Act to Control the Controllable. How about you? Is worry prompting you to take action? For instance, is worrying about your child's education prompting you to meet with their teacher? Is worrying about money prompting you to see a financial advisor, to begin tracking your spending to see where your money is really going, or to get advice from a colleague on how to build your business? Is worrying about having too much to do prompting you to ask for support, to leave some things undone, or to learn how to say "no"? Is worrying about your health prompting you to take better care of yourself or to see a doctor? When worry is prompting you to take action, this step of the CALM process has the tools you need! Read on to learn how to craft an action plan that will help you act in the presence of fear, reduce the toll of stress on your body and mind, make value-based decisions, and take courageous action.

CHAPTER 7

Craft Your Action Plan

How to Use Worry to Your Advantage

Mary Hemingway said, "Worry a little bit every day and in a lifetime you will lose a couple of years. If something is wrong, fix it if you can. But train yourself not to worry. Worry never fixes anything." Isn't that good advice? In other words, take action to control the things you can and learn to let the rest go. To fix what you can, start by identifying what needs fixing.

In this case, what's been worrying you? Take a moment to write it down and be as specific as possible. For example, let's say you're worried about work. What specifically about work is worrying you? Is it the hours? If so, keep digging. What specifically is it about the hours? Are you worried about still being at work while the kids are home alone after school? Keep digging. What specifically are you worried about when it comes to the kids being home alone after school?

What you're doing by doing this is getting to the root of your worry. Once that root is exposed, you have the information you need to create an action plan to control the things you can. And having an action plan does wonders for reducing worry and stress. Once you've identified your concerns, use these three brainstorming questions to help you craft your action plan:

- ¤ **"Who could I ask?"**
- ¤ **"What could I do?"**
- ¤ **"What could I read?"**

With those questions in mind, can you think of any actions you can take to control the controllable when it comes to the things you're worried about? If something comes to mind, write it down. A written action plan helps to keep you focused and on track. You may also find it helpful to join forces with a partner to brainstorm a list of possible actions that your worries might be prompting you to take. If one question prompts more answers than another, that's fine. These questions are meant to help you, not create more worry!

What if you think there are no actions you can take in your situation? Rest assured that the possibility of improving your situation by taking action almost always exists—even in the direst of circumstances. In fact, taking action—using those exact three questions—helped me to get out of a pit of serious depression. Here's how I got out from that dark place and how you—or someone you may know who is feeling this way—can get out too!

A Case Study: My Story of Recovery

A few years ago, I lost the joy I used to get from doing things that once mattered to me. I felt alone. I felt hopeless. I couldn't see any light at the end of the tunnel. There was a part of me that wasn't quite sure I could survive this seemingly unbearable pain.

I also felt embarrassed, and I was worried about being judged. *I can't tell people I'm depressed,* I thought. *I'm the Worry Management Expert. I'm not supposed to be feeling this way.* Yet I *was* feeling this way—and the pain and shame were preventing me from taking action to do anything about it.

During this time, my friend Doug sent a text to me asking if I could meet with him for a coffee. Doug has been a colleague of mine for over fifteen years. He's also one of my very best friends and just so happens to be the lead pastor of my church. I accepted his invitation, and we met at his office. Even now, I find that space very comforting. It reminds me of a peaceful library with its floor-to-ceiling shelves, filled to the brim with neatly organized books. On that day, we sat down at his desk with our coffees, and Doug asked, "On a scale of one to ten, where do you feel your life is at right now?"

I burst into tears and replied, "One." I'd been feeling depressed for months, and this was the first time I had admitted it to anyone.

"Oh, I would have given you at least a four," he said gently.

That made me smile through my tears. I'd known my friend truly cared about me, but in that moment, I actually felt his concern. *I'm not on my own,* I thought. *I don't have to hide this depression any longer.*

Mama Bear, what are you hiding? Are you hiding feelings of depression, like I was? Are you hiding feelings of resentment, overwhelm, or anger? Are you covering up an addiction, eating disorder, or other problem because you're worried about what other people would think of you if they found out? What is it?

Whatever it is, I guarantee that you're not the only one feeling this way. You're not the only one going through what you're going through. It's okay. You're okay. You're not alone, and it's not hopeless.

Admitting to yourself—and to someone you trust—what's really going on for you takes courage but it also sets you free. In finally being honest about how I was feeling, I freed myself from the inner turmoil that hiding the depression was causing me. I freed myself from feeling embarrassed about my emotions or afraid of being judged. This freedom created just enough space for hope to enter my life. That tiny spark of hope helped me to believe that joy could return and that I could begin moving forward.

Being open about what is really going on for you is an important first step in crafting an action plan—especially if you've been hiding your true feelings. If people are trying to hide or ignore a problem, or if they feel hopeless about ever finding a solution, they tend to not take action to resolve it. Mama Bear, getting the truth out into the open puts you in a much better position to start moving forward. It can serve as the foundation from which you can create a powerful action plan.

A Note on Depression: You're Not Alone

Mama Bear, I want to be very clear on something. If you're struggling with your mental health, it does not make you a bad mom. I know what it's like to feel embarrassed, what it's like to think, *If I was stronger, I'd be better.* But those thoughts aren't true. Needing support with your mental health does not make you weak; it makes you human.

There are many times in a mom's life during which she may experience depression. Many moms experience postpartum depression after their babies are born, and a review of recent literature shows that up to 40 percent of mothers experience postpartum anxiety.[7] Moms also often experience situational depression during difficult life experiences like separation, divorce, serious illness in the family, or becoming an empty nester. Some

> Depression is common—and it's serious—but it's *treatable.* If you think you may be depressed, don't hesitate to tell someone.

moms feel depressed every year during the winter months due to seasonal affective disorder. Others may experience what is known as chronic depression, which may not have a clear cause or timing. But the types of depression matter less than this fact: Depression is common—and it's serious—but it's *treatable.* If you think you may be depressed, don't hesitate to tell someone. Seek immediate treatment from your health care provider. There's always help and hope!

Moving Forward with Hope

Now that I was no longer hiding how I was feeling, after that meeting with Doug, I was able to create an action plan to care for my mental health. I asked myself, "Who could I ask for help? What could I do next? What could I read now?" Then I answered, "I could tell my sister how I'm feeling. I could use extra love and support."

So I called her. I told her exactly how I'd been feeling: "I understand now how it feels for people when they get to that low point where they feel hopeless and think about ending their life," I said through my tears. "But don't worry. I'm not going to do that."

"I'm proud of you for telling me how you're feeling," my sister said. "Don't ever end your life. It doesn't stop the pain; it just passes the pain on to the people who love you."

I could not imagine passing the pain I was in onto my kids. I thought, *If I have to suffer with this pain for the rest of my life so they don't have to suffer, that's what I'm willing to do.*

But Mama Bear, having experienced depression firsthand, I've learned that you don't have to suffer. Instead, you can take the action of asking for help. I understand that it's hard to reach out for help when you're feeling that way. I know it takes courage. Start with taking one small step.

My next step was to find a good therapist. *Hmmmmm,* I thought. *I'll check back with my friend Doug. He's an international speaker like me and a pastor. Surely he'll know of a good therapist.* He did! The therapist he recommended for me turned out to be an incredibly helpful piece of my recovery.

I then took the action of seeing my family physician. He recommended antidepressants to help me get through this difficult time. (Medication may also be an option for you to discuss with your health care provider. Just as you might need a cast while you heal from a broken bone, you also might need medication while you get treatment for any mental health issues.)

By this point, the depression was lifting, but I continued asking myself, "What could I do? What could I read? Who could I ask?" (By the way, you can ask and answer these questions in whichever order works best for you. It's not even necessary for you to have answers for each question. They are simply prompts to guide you to possible actions you could take.)

I talked with my friend Larry, who suggested I meet up with a friend of his for coffee. *I really don't feel like meeting new people right now,* I thought at first. *But Larry thinks I have a lot in common with this woman and that we could end up being good friends. I need to keep moving forward. Okay, I'll do it.*

I met with Larry's friend at a little European bakery around the corner from my house. During the conversation, she shared with me the deep emotional pain she'd endured after her father had died.

"The sadness felt unbearable," she said. "Then one day, the grief just lifted. It was like the storm suddenly stopped and the sun came out. You have to keep holding on during the storm because one day it will suddenly end." That statement touched my soul. I felt immense hope that someday my sadness would suddenly end too.

I asked her, "Did you do anything to help lift the grief?"

"Yes," she said. "I started focusing more on being grateful."

Wait a minute, I thought. At some point, someone had recommended I read the book *The Five-Minute Journal*.[8] This book includes list prompts designed to help people focus on the positives in their lives for a few minutes each morning and evening. I decided I could take action and pick up a copy for myself.

I bought the book right after our coffee meeting. While I read it, and after, I did as the book suggested, spending time every day focusing on gratitude. As a result, I began experiencing a huge shift! The more thankful I became, the more positive I felt. After determining who I could ask, what I could do, and what I could read—and following through on those actions—the speed at which my life turned around was nothing short of miraculous.

Today, I can honestly say that I am fulfilled! I have vision, clarity, and purpose. I wake up filled with gratitude for my life. I'm not exaggerating. My first waking thoughts are of thanks. I'm thankful for the work I'm blessed to do. I wake up in the morning brimming with excitement about the possibilities for the day ahead.

I am fortunate that I no longer require antidepressants. I'm no longer just alive: breathing, surviving, going through the motions. I'm full of life: thriving, working, playing, and smiling, with joy, peace, and gratitude in my heart.

Looking back, I'm thankful for the season of difficulty I endured. Through that experience, I was strengthened and equipped. It provided me with a deep understanding of what others may feel during their own seasons of difficulty. I know what it's like for people who feel like they've lost hope, and I know how to help them find their way out of that dark place. Sometimes all you need—like I did—is just that little spark of hope to help you take a first step and a second step and then a third, out of the darkness and into the light.

Mama Bear, remember that different degrees and types of depression require different treatments. Be confident that you are taking the right steps and doing all the right things you need in order to look after yourself and your precious kids. Regardless of your current situation—no matter how insurmountable it seems—you can succeed. You can move beyond surviving and begin thriving in an extraordinary life. Whatever has been weighing you down, stressing you out, or keeping you up at night with worry, now is the time for you to craft your own action plan to control the controllable. Ask yourself, "Who could I ask? What could I do? What could I read?"

Ask Yourself: Who Could I Ask?

Asking someone else for their opinion, recommendation, or advice can work wonders to calm a worried mind. One conversation could lead to ideas, insights, and solutions you might not have thought of on your own, just like talking to my friend Doug, my sister, my therapist, and my physician helped me with the next steps in my action plan.

However, it's important you select the *right* person to go to. Otherwise, that conversation could end in even more stress and upset feelings then you had before you asked.

For example, a mom once posted a question in a Facebook group for parents. "Help," she said. "I'm at my wits' end. My toddler was sleeping through the night. For the last two weeks he has been getting up every night and crying. I'm exhausted, and I don't know what to do. Any advice?"

A battle between moms began about the appropriate course of action this tired Mama Bear *should* take. You know, it's time we remove the word "should" from our vocabulary. As moms, we need to stop "should-ing on ourselves" and other mothers. Yes, I know what that phrase sounds like. Yet it's kind of "apro-poo," don't you think? Sorry, not sorry.

Some of the online moms offered empathy and encouraged her to "hang in there." Some moms gave well-intentioned advice based on their own experiences with their children. Other moms harshly criticized the offered advice, and the well-intentioned moms defended themselves. Arguments ensued. Comments were deleted. And in the end, I have a feeling that this tired Mama Bear was even more at her wits' end than she was before she asked for a second opinion.

Many conversations with well-intentioned yet misguided people can end in a similar experience. For that reason, it's wise to be selective about whose opinion you seek. Here are four ways to ensure you're asking the right person for advice:

¤ **Talk to an expert.** Is this person an expert in the area you need support in? When it comes to diapers, family meal suggestions, and the best name for your kids' new goldfish, it's fine to go to a social media parenting group to ask other moms—who you've never met before—for advice. In many cases, support and encouragement from other moms can be helpful. However, sometimes what you need is an expert. If you're worried that your child is unwell, ask a doctor. If you're going through a separation and need legal advice, ask a family lawyer. If you're worried that your child might be struggling at school, ask their teacher. When expert advice is what you need, ask an expert.

¤ **Choose someone you trust.** Is this person someone you trust? Is it someone who wants the best for you? You need to feel comfortable that your go-to person is someone you trust and who has your best interests at heart. If you ask this individual to keep the conversation between the two of you, do you believe they will do so? Here's one way to determine whether someone will keep your confidence: listen to how they speak about others to you. If this person usually speaks highly of others and doesn't tend to gossip, that's a pretty good indication that you can count on this person to keep your confidence and speak highly of you too.

¤ **Beware of your "worry buddy."** Is this person your worry buddy? A worry buddy is that person you call to tell them what you're worried about, to which they most often say, "Oh, no! That's terrible!" Together you feed into the worry and cause it to grow. You want to make sure your go-to person is someone who worries at least a little less than you do. This doesn't mean you can't speak to your worry buddy when you're stressed. A good friend can provide you with a certain amount of encouragement and reassurance when you need it. If that's what you need, make sure that is exactly what you ask for. Say "I need some encouragement today" or "I just want your reassurance that everything is going to be okay." Reassurance and encouragement can go a long way in easing a worried mind. However, when you really need a true assessment of your situation—or that expert advice—consider seeking advice from a different individual.

¤ **Choose an optimistic thinker.** Does this person tend to have an optimistic outlook? Steer clear of asking negative thinkers for their perspective on your circumstances. A negative force can have such a strong pull that you might find yourself even more confused and frustrated than you were before you asked for a second opinion. And by "optimistic thinker," I'm not talking about someone who provides false flattery or misleading reassurance. I'm talking about someone who can help you to see the most hopeful view in any situation while still keeping the facts in mind.

Ask Yourself: What Could I Do?

In my situation, I took the action of being honest with people about how I was feeling. Now let's look at your own situation—and your own list of worries: what could you do? Here are some things to keep in mind while you answer that question:

¤ **Be bold and think big.** Sometimes when creating your action plan, you might be tempted to censor your ideas because taking action can be scary. But this initial stage is simply a brainstorming session, so you don't have to be afraid. Coming up in the next chapter, you'll learn how to overcome fears and roadblocks that can stop you from taking action, but for right now, your mission is to come up with as many possible actions as you can. Go ahead— be bold and think big!

¤ **Be creative.** Creativity will be particularly important if you're worried about something that is beyond your control: the economy, the weather, and your in-laws are just a few that come to mind. However, with a little ingenuity and some creative thinking, you'll be amazed at what actions you can come up with to influence things you think are uncontrollable. Take people, for example. Can you control another person's behavior? If your child has ever had a temper tantrum on the grocery store floor, you'll know the answer to that question is a resounding "No!" However, it is possible—not necessarily easy, but possible—to *influence* another's behavior. I've taught full-day seminars about dealing with difficult people, so I know if you take the initiative of changing your own behavior, you can influence another's behavior to change as well.

¤ **Focus on what you can do.** For instance, imagine you're planning an outdoor birthday party for your child, and you're worried that it might rain, spoiling the event. Rather than focusing on what you can't do (control the weather), shift your attention to what you can do. In this scenario, you could create an indoor backup plan, arrange for tents, or schedule an alternate date. Taking these actions will influence the success of the event—and put your mind at ease in the meantime—rain or shine. Here's another example. Suppose you're worried about your teenager getting into a car accident while driving on the highway during the winter. You can't control the other drivers. You can't control the weather. What can you do? You can influence how your vehicle drives in the cold, snow, rain, or ice by making sure your car is equipped with the proper tires. You can influence how your child handles poor weather conditions by having your teen take a defensive driving course. Some things are unquestionably beyond your control, and you can either be reactive and let the outcome influence you or you can be proactive and influence the outcome for yourself. When you're writing down your action plan, focus on the actions you can take. The key is to focus on what you can do, not on what you can't.

Ask Yourself: What Could I Read?

When I was suffering with depression, I read *The Five-Minute Journal.* What book do you need to read (or reread) right now? Reading can help you solve your biggest challenges and gain your greatest victories by providing you with ideas to include in your action plan.

Worried about your relationship with your child? The right book could give you strategies on how to really connect with your kid. Worried about your finances? The right book could help you with methods to generate multiple streams of income, to budget wisely, to buy your first house, or to build your business.

Humans are creatures of habit. Even our thoughts are habitual. Did you know that most of the thoughts you think today are the same thoughts you thought yesterday, and the thoughts you had yesterday were mostly the same thoughts you had the day before that? Reading can give you *new* ideas. Reading gives you the chance to fill your mind with new thoughts that lead to new feelings that lead to new actions for your action plan.

World-renowned business speaker and author Jim Rohn said, "Reading is essential for those who seek to rise above the ordinary. We must not permit anything to stand between us and the book that could change our lives." From this point forward, don't let anything stand between you and the book that could change your life! Here are some pointers to start off your search:

¤ **Determine what you need.** What area of your life do you need the most inspiration, ideas, or insights in? This includes the area of your life that is currently causing you the most distress, discomfort, or anxiety. If you're not sure, revisit what you listed as a concern or worry at the beginning of this section and consider starting there.

¤ **Select a book and read it.** Think about that area you need the most assistance with—parenting, potty training, dog training, building a happy family, whatever. If you can name it, somebody likely wrote a book about it. Search your favorite bookstore or library website for books on that topic (or ask friends for recommendations) and pick one that seems like a solid source. Write the title down in your action plan and make a commitment to download, purchase, or borrow it, and then read it.

¤ **Capture the ideas.** While you're reading, write down the ideas and insights you uncover directly into your action plan. At first glance, this may seem like a lot of work. But consider how many times we take the time to read, get inspired, discover something new, and then completely forget what we learned. Capturing the strategies you learn by writing them down will allow you to remember later those words and ideas that are most important to you now.

Creating an action plan gives you concrete steps to take to address your worries and better your life. Taking action to fix the things you can control is a way to use worry to your advantage. When you take action to control the things you can, you are no longer a servant to worry. Instead, worry is now serving you! When this flip happens, worry loses its grip on you, and you become free. Free to make decisions with greater ease. Free to move forward with more confidence. Free to live and parent with greater peace and deeper joy!

Take a Break—What Do You Think?

Take five or ten minutes right now to craft an action plan. Are your worries prompting you to take action? What actions can you take to control the controllable? Ask yourself, "Who could I ask? What could I do? What could I read?" Write down your answers to those three questions as they come. Remember to write them on paper, think big, and be creative. Creating an action plan—and following through on that action plan—can transform obstacles into opportunities and worries into inner peace.

CHAPTER 8

Overcome Fears

The Emotional Roadblocks on Your Action Journey and Remedies for Moving through Them

Erma Bombeck said, "Worry is like a rocking chair; it gives you something to do but it never gets you anywhere." Do you know what will get you somewhere? Taking action to control the things you can!

So far in this part of the book, you've learned that sometimes worry is actually prompting you to take action. You've discovered three questions to help craft your action plan—"Who could I ask? What could I do? What could I read?"—and how to brainstorm steps for that plan. Now it's time to take action. Sounds simple enough, right?

Unfortunately, the challenge here is that fear, doubt, and worry can arise at just the thought of following through on our action plans. In fact, here's how most attempts to take action go down—especially those requiring us to step outside of our comfort zones. You want to take action, and you have a plan to do so, but you worry:

- ¤ "What if I fail?"
- ¤ "What if I get rejected?"
- ¤ "What if I make a mistake?"
- ¤ "What if I can't do it?"
- ¤ "What if I'm not good enough?"

Look at your own life. Have fear, doubt, or worry ever stopped you from taking action? Really think about it. Have you ever avoided doing something because you worried what other people would think of you? Have you ever stopped yourself from moving forward because you doubted you could succeed? Have you ever given up because you feared rejection?

Fear, doubt, and worry can be the biggest obstacles to following through on our action plans. In this section, we're going to look at some of the most common emotional roadblocks that stop people from taking action—and the remedies for overcoming those roadblocks.

Roadblock: Fear of Rejection

When I was looking for a publisher for my first book, I walked through years of rejection. It started with literary agents: I'd submit my proposal, get rejected, submit my proposal, and get rejected again. But that's okay, because I love rejection . . . said no one ever!

Back then, I had a lot riding on securing a book deal. Doing so would allow me to continue to set my own work hours, which meant I could drive my kids to and from school and dance classes and be there for them when they needed help with homework, personal issues, or anything in between. I also needed to make money—not working simply wasn't an option. Most importantly, publishing a book was one of my big dreams. But with each rejection, I felt closer and closer to losing that dream.

Have you felt the sting of rejection? Rejection is one of those uncontrollable things in life. You can't control other people. You can't control how and what other people think and feel. You can't force someone to want what it is you have to offer. But what you can control is your ability to keep moving forward in the face of rejection. How? One way is to avoid taking the rejection personally.

Remedy: Avoid Taking It Personally

Some rejections feel incredibly personal. Say, for instance, your child decides he is officially too old to hug you in front of his friends, and he dodges you when you try. That can hurt. Yet when you really examine what's happening, you can see it's not about you. It's about your child growing and setting boundaries based on what he feels is right for him. Looking at it from that perspective, you can feel good about the job you're doing as his parent. You've raised him to trust his own wants and needs. When you avoid taking things personally, it helps you to adapt to changes faster and to keep moving forward.

Even though it really felt like the literary agents were rejecting me, the thing that helped keep me going was to remember it wasn't me they were rejecting—it was my proposal. Once you've realized that it's not personal, how do you keep moving forward? You can do so by answering the same three questions you used to create your action plan: "Who could I ask? What could I do? What could I read?"

To keep moving forward with my goal of getting published, I read *Write the Perfect Book Proposal: 10 That Sold and Why*[9]. Using the ideas in that book, I improved my book proposal a lot! Now all I had to do was find the right literary agent. I thought the right literary agent would be the one who represented very successful authors, so I looked for some. There was one author I had in mind who, at the time, was selling millions of books. I read one of his acknowledgment sections, and sure enough, he thanked his literary agent in it.

Aha, I thought. *That's who I want! I'm coming after you. But how do I stand out from the thousands of other authors submitting their proposals?*

After I figured out what to do, I acted on my plan. I made a mock cover of my book on my computer. I printed it out and wrapped it around another book that I figured was the same size mine would be once I'd finished writing it. Then I took the book to a bookstore. I put the book on a shelf under the "Self-Help" sign and took a panoramic picture of it. I had the picture developed, put it in a nice black frame, and wrapped it in gold Christmas paper (because it was just before Christmas).

I boxed that picture up to send to the literary agency, and with it I included a handwritten note saying, "You won't recognize the title of the book in this picture. That's because it hasn't been published yet, but you don't want to be the agent kicking yourself for not getting the commission when it's on the best-seller list." Then I sent the package to that agency in Texas.

About a month later, I got a call from one of the agents working in the firm. When my cell phone rang, I was standing in front of Cinderella's castle in Disney World with my husband and two daughters.

The agent introduced himself and said, "Tell me about yourself. What is this book about?" We spoke for around an hour, and at the end of the call, he said he'd represent me. Woo-hoo! And just before hanging up, he said, "By the way, I thought this was a Christmas present."

I said, "It was! Merry Christmas!"

The call ended, and I looked up at Cinderella's castle and started jumping up and down, saying "I did it! I did it!" My girls jumped up and down with me. What a great example for your children, right? To see the results of their mom persevering despite obstacles. It strengthens their minds with the belief that they can keep moving forward with their dreams too.

Three months after that phone call, I received a handwritten note from my agent. He'd tried nine different publishers, and the proposal had been rejected by all nine. He wrote, "Denise, I was unsuccessful in finding a home for your project. I would love to work on something with you in the future. Keep me posted."

Ah, man. Rejected? Again? I thought I was going to get it this time! What am I going to do? And wait . . . nine?

He rejected me after he received only nine rejections. But nine is not enough rejections to measure success or failure. Can you imagine if you had given up on dating, parenting, or anything else you really wanted after only nine rejections?

I knew what I had to do. I had to fire my literary agent. But I didn't. I held on.

Roadblock: Worrying about What Other People Think

One of the main reasons I held on was because I'd already told people about my new awesome literary agent from Texas. I didn't want my friends and family to think I had failed. So, instead, I held on to that agent. Even though he was no longer trying to find a publisher for my book, I held on.

Have you ever avoided telling people what was happening or how you were really feeling because you worried too much about what they might think of you? Have you ever stopped yourself from taking action on something that was important to you because you were worried about being judged or criticized? When you worry about what other people think, that worry can keep you stuck.

I was keeping myself stuck because I cared too much about what other people thought of me. I had experienced so much rejection from people—throughout my entire life—that I had incorrectly tied my identity to the success of my business. I thought, *If I get a book deal, people will view me as a success, which means I am a success. If I don't get a book deal, people will view me as a failure, which means I am a failure.*

Can you see how sneaky assumptions can be? Assuming how others will view me based on a book deal is a pretty big—and incorrect—assumption. And just as you can make incorrect assumptions about how others see you, others can guess wrong about you too. Just because some people view you a certain way doesn't make their opinion true. Besides, the people who love you will continue to love you regardless of the success of your business, the choices you make, or the bumps you encounter along the way. It's time to stop trying to please everybody and to begin caring about yourself.

Remedy: Care More about What You Think of Yourself

You always have the choice between caring about what others think of you and caring about what you think of yourself. I strongly recommend that you choose you. Don't sacrifice your life trying to please others. Act and move forward.

Eleven months and thirteen days after I'd received the rejection notice from my literary agent, I went to see a movie with my husband. The movie was *Runaway Jury*. In one scene in the movie, one of the lead characters said to another, "Call Mr. [So-and-so]. Tell him his service is no longer required."

The character said the exact name of my agent. This name had come up in the movie neither before that point nor after it. I turned to my husband and said, "Did you hear that?"

With a look of amazement on his face, he said, "Yes!"

In that moment, I finally let go. I let go of worrying about what other people might think of me by choosing to care more about what I thought of myself. That's when I became free. I became free of the fear, and I became free to take action. I'd been holding on for far too long—eleven months and thirteen days too long, to be exact. I sent the literary agent a letter terminating the author-agent agreement the very next day.

Let me ask you this: What have you been holding onto for too long? Is it fear? Is it worry about what other people think? What do you need to let go of to move forward and start caring about yourself?

By letting go of my worry about others' opinions, I was finally free to move forward. I thought, *You know what? I'm going to do this myself. I'm cutting out the middleman and going to publishers on my own.* I started submitting my proposal directly to publishers. And . . . I experienced another year of rejection. I was bewildered. I thought, *Something's got to be wrong with my proposal.*

What do you do when you experience a roadblock while taking action? Do you give up? You sure don't! You keep going by again asking yourself: "Who could I ask? What could I do? What could I read?"

And that's exactly what I did. My answer? *I'll ask my friend Nick.*

Roadblock: Fear of Criticism

My friend Nick is a best-selling author. He kind of reminds me of a tall Hugh Grant. He's very distinguished, and he's got that posh British accent too. He also just so happens to be very direct. He doesn't sugarcoat his words. He just tells it like he sees it. It was going to take courage for me to ask Nick for his opinion because it meant I was inviting criticism.

I certainly understand how hard it can be to follow through on your action plan when faced with the possibility of being criticized. However, being willing to listen to constructive criticism can help you to make massive strides forward in life. I mustered up all the courage I could, and I invited Nick for a bite to eat.

We met for lunch at this cute little museum café. There were brightly colored abstract paintings hanging on the walls, and soothing music whispered through the sound system. After some small talk, I shared my recent book-publishing challenges with Nick. He looked at my proposal and bluntly observed, "I know what's wrong with your book."

"What is it?"

"It has a rotten title."

Ouch! Criticism is about as much fun as a root canal.

Remedy: Consider the Source

> Constructive criticism can help you to grow, but judgmental criticism has got to go!

Here's a good rule of thumb to follow when criticism comes your way: Constructive criticism can help you to grow, but judgmental criticism has got to go! How do you determine whether the feedback you're receiving is constructive or judgmental?

You consider the source.

Who is criticizing you? Is it someone you trust, someone who wants the best for you? What gives this person credibility? I chose to ask for and listen to Nick's advice because he was a best-selling author of several books. This means he had experience in the area I was seeking advice about. He had a proven track record. He had credibility. So I asked him why he thought it was a rotten title, to which he quickly replied, "Nobody can say it."

He was right. The original title of my book was *From Worrier to Warrior.* I'd been giving seminars with the same title, and at times the people who introduced me would stumble when they tried to say it. Sometimes they would say, "From Worrier to Worrier"—so there will be no change in how you feel after hearing this presentation, right? Other times, introducers would say, "From Warrior to Worrier," which is even worse.

Nick's critique was difficult to hear, but because I knew Nick had a history of success, I trusted him and accepted what he was telling me.

Roadblock: Self-Doubt

So I needed to change the title. While I was brainstorming new ones, I also thought, *If the title is that bad, maybe the entire book is too. What if I can't do this after all?* There it is—our good friend self-doubt.

What are you afraid of? Do you ever face the fear of not being good enough, smart enough, or worthy enough? That feeling of self-doubt can be a huge stumbling block as you are trying to take action to control the things you can, because it tells you that you aren't capable of doing so.

Don't let the thing that stops you be you. You *are* good enough. You are smart enough. You are worthy. Break free from the shackles of self-doubt by focusing on what you can do!

Remedy: Focus on What You Can Do

Focusing on what you can do will help you to let go of that defeatist mentality. To shake off self-doubt and regain your focus, declare, "Of course I can do this. I am strong. I can handle it. I am resourceful. I can succeed!"

Instead of doubting my book, I became laser focused on what I could do. I told myself, "I can keep going. I can succeed. I can think of a new name for my book." Then I thought, *Wait a minute! The entire book is built around the acronym CALM. How did I not see this before? I'll call the book "CALM: A Proven Four-Step Process Designed Specifically for Women Who Worry."* I changed the title in my proposal, packaged it up, and sent it off to one of the largest publishers of self-help books in all of North America.

One month later, I received an email from the publishing house. Before I opened it, I didn't expect much. For years I had opened emails, and all I had seen were rejections. However, this time I opened the email, and it was from the publisher's CEO. He said that he was interested in my book idea and his assistant would be in touch to arrange a time for us to talk!

The day of the call, I was so nervous. It felt like this was make-or-break time. I got on the phone with the CEO, and he asked me questions about the book and about who I was. Then he said, "We'd like to publish your book." Mama Bear, I changed the title of my book and my dream came true! Let that sink in as a reminder: Keep moving forward! You could be only one small adjustment away from everything coming together for you too.

In that moment, I felt as happy as the titular character of *Ted Lasso* when he said, "I tell ya, man. I feel like we fell out of a lucky tree, hit every branch on the way down, ended up in a pool full of cash and Sour Patch Kids."[10] Then it dawned on me: *Wait, all of those rejections over the years weren't failures. They were catapults to this moment.* The rejections you have faced in your past aren't failures! They are simply stepping stones to success.

Keep Moving Forward

All those years when I was facing rejection and opening myself up to constructive criticism, I was growing. I was learning from mistakes and continuing to move forward. I wasn't keeping myself stuck anymore; I was becoming unstoppable. Finally finding a publisher for my book was a pivotal moment. You'll experience this too as you continue to take action despite your fear. As you continue to act and move forward in the face of doubt, fear, and rejection, you'll get stronger, and you'll become an unstoppable action-taker.

What have you been putting on hold because fear is getting in the way? Listen, everyone feels afraid at one time or another. Some people are afraid of failure, while others are afraid of success. Some are afraid of not standing out, and others are afraid of not fitting in. It's okay. Fear is a natural emotion. However, if fear is getting in the way of taking action to accomplish something important to you, don't let it. Do the thing you're afraid of. You just might find that what you were afraid of isn't as bad as you imagined it would be.

What actions are your worries prompting you to take? Create your action plan by asking yourself, "Who could I ask? What could I do? What could I read?" Then act and move forward—even in the presence of fear.

When you're fearing rejection, avoid taking it personally. When you're worried about what other people think, choose to care more about what you think of yourself. If you're afraid of criticism, consider the source. To break free from self-doubt, focus on what you can do. Above all—keep moving forward!

Let's keep moving forward in this book too. With the remedies to these roadblocks in hand, it's time to move on to the next chapter and learn ways to reduce the physical and emotional effects of stress and worry.

> ### Take a Break: An Affirmation
>
> Mama Bear, when you find yourself worrying about what other people think of you, try this old Gaelic blessing on for size:
>
> *May those who love us, love us*
>
> *And those that don't love us, may God turn their hearts;*
>
> *And if he doesn't turn their hearts, may he turn their ankles*
>
> *So we'll know them by their limping.*

CHAPTER 9

Reduce the Physical and Emotional Effects of Stress and Worry

The Doable Dozen for Mama Bear's Self-Care

I magine you're holding a rubber band. You take the rubber band, and you begin to stretch it. If you continue to stretch it beyond its maximum tension point, what will happen? It will eventually break. It will snap. Sometimes moms and rubber bands have more in common than we'd like to think.

Have you ever felt like a rubber band? Have you ever felt stretched and pulled in so many directions that you felt you were going to snap at any moment? Of course you have—you're a parent! This maximum tension point, or "snapping" point, is different for everyone because we each have our own unique tolerance level for stress.

Is it wrong to stretch yourself? Not at all. By stretching yourself, you discover how far you can truly go. However, when you live your life continually stretched out—and stressed out—to your maximum tension point, there isn't a lot of room for fun, and you run the risk of snapping. It's much easier to release the pressure on a stretched rubber band than it is to fix a broken one. If you feel that you're approaching your snapping point, this section will explore ways to help you ease the tension and regain a more relaxed state.

Do you have mixed feelings about self-care, Mama Bear? Some moms have told me they feel selfish taking care of their own needs. Others have told me that desperately needing time for themselves makes them feel like they are doing something wrong or that they're failing as moms.

Let's address that right now. Taking time for yourself doesn't make you a bad mom; it makes you human. Being a mom is awesome, *and* it's hard. The physical work that comes along with parenting can be exhausting—the cleaning, refereeing, chauffeuring, cooking, lifting, carrying, boo-boo kissing, and helping with homework and broken hearts. But it's not just the physical work that weighs on us. The mental and emotional load is heavy to bear as well. I remember someone telling me, "When your kids are little, it's hard physical work. When they're older, it's hard emotional work." In the midst of all that, of course, you need a break!

Self-care will help you to regain strength and vitality. When you take care of yourself, you'll be able to parent with more energy, joy, and peace. When Mama Bear is doing well, the family does well. Here are twelve ideas to help you recharge physically, emotionally, mentally, and spiritually.

1—Reduce Noise Triggers: Ask yourself, "Where can I turn down the volume in my environment today?"

Why is noise so triggering? Mom life is already overstimulating. The whining, random ear-piercing screams, beeping toys, rambunctious playtime, arguing, loud electronics, music practice—all of this noise can add to feelings of anxiety and overwhelm.

I remember days when I thought, *If I hear the word "Mom" one more time, I'm going to lose it!* On a few occasions, I asked my kids to call me Denise for an hour. For that hour, it was like I was working at an office populated by small coworkers who don't close the bathroom door. *I really need to talk to the boss about that. Oh, wait. That's me!*

Kidding aside, I needed a break from hearing the word "Mom." Can you relate? What kind of mother gets tired of hearing her child say "Mom"? I'll tell you what kind: a good one!

To reduce noise triggers, lower the volume on the television and on handheld devices. Turn down the music. Try talking quietly to reduce your *own* noise level. If you have a child in the house who practices an instrument, try wearing earplugs. You'll still be able to hear through them, but the sound barrier will help cut down on some of the noise. When possible, take a quiet break by yourself. Music and yelling are fun to listen to during halftime at a football game, but you don't want to feel like your eardrums—and your emotions—are in a never-ending marching band. All moms benefit from a little "Mama Bear Quiet Time."

2—Nurture Yourself in Nature: Ask yourself, "How am I getting outside today?"

In his book *Keep Sharp: Build a Better Brain at Any Age*, Dr. Sanjay Gupta writes about *shinrin-yoku*, also called Japanese forest bathing. *Shinrin-yoku* means "just being in the presence of trees," Gupta writes.

> *Forest bathing has been popular lately as a way to lower heart rate and blood pressure and reduce stress hormone production. When you are forest bathing and breathing in the "aroma of the forest," you are also absorbing substances known as phytoncides, which protect trees from insects and other stressors. As we have learned over the past decade, these phytoncides can also protect us by increasing our natural killer immune cells and decreasing cortisol levels. While spending time in nature or green spaces has long been recommended to improve mental well-being, we now understand what that aroma of the forest is really doing for our bodies and brains. You needn't travel to a far-off forest; you can do well by yourself just by digging in the dirt of your own garden or visiting a local park.*[11]

Nurture yourself in nature to calm your mind, reduce stress, and lower cortisol levels. If you take your littles with you, you can teach them how to breathe the "aroma of the forest" in—even if you're doing so while wandering the small community park around the corner or digging in the dirt around the city-planted tree near the sidewalk.

3—Reduce Mess Triggers: Ask yourself, "What three items of clutter can I decide today to discard, donate, recycle, or sell?"

Why is mess so triggering? The stress of mess can make it difficult to relax, and when there's clutter and disorder, it can be hard to think clearly. On top of that, disorganization makes tackling regular daily tasks more difficult. Searching through all the stuff to find what you need—like your cell phone, your car keys, or your child's field trip permission form—is time consuming and stressful. Sometimes mess is triggering because of a faulty belief system: "If I were a good mom, my house would be clean," we tell ourselves. At other times, we feel stressed by mess because we just don't know where to begin.

Here's a good place to start. In the next twenty-four hours, get rid of three items of clutter. Clutter is anything you no longer need, use, or love. Can you choose three items of clutter to throw out, donate, or recycle right now? Accomplishing this small goal will help you get over the most challenging hurdle of decluttering—getting started.

The next thing you could do is take four empty boxes and label them "Discard," "Donate," "Recycle," and "Sell." Over the course of each day, when you come across things that you no longer need, use, or love, put them in the appropriate box. Take the Donate box to the charity shop when it's full. Take the Discard and Recycle items to the curb on garbage day. When you have the time to do so, sell the items you feel may have monetary value.

Occasionally, you'll come across an item you no longer need, use, or love, but you'll still hesitate to part with it because of this common thought: *What if I need it someday?* Resist it. This what-if question is a clutter-creator!

Ask yourself this question instead: "When was the last time I actually used this item?" Experts say that if you haven't used an item in the past twelve to eighteen months, chances are pretty good that you won't need it in the future. All of the seasons have passed by, and you haven't used it.

You might ask, "What if I plan on having another child? Are you saying that if I haven't used baby items (like a crib, stroller, or baby clothes) in twelve to eighteen months, I should get rid of them?" Not at all. Those items would fall into the need-use-love category. In this case, you know your plans are to have another child, and so you need those items. Remember, clutter is anything that you no longer need, use, or love.

Now the day may come when you discover that you got rid of something you could have used. However, instead of allowing that experience to stop you from future decluttering, answer this question: "Would I have known where to find it—or even remembered I owned it—if I hadn't discovered it while decluttering in the first place?"

As you build momentum and continue to clear your space, you'll be amazed at how calm, clear, and relaxed your mind will become.

4—Tickle Your Funny Bone: Ask yourself, "How can I add laughter to my day today?"

Jasper Carrott said, "Laughter is the best medicine—unless you're diabetic, then insulin comes pretty high on the list." Laughter really is good medicine. It causes your body to release endorphins—the body's natural painkiller! Laughter also helps to reduce cortisol, the stress hormone.

What makes you laugh? Look for ways to add humor to your life. Watch a comedy, share a funny video, or post silly photos. Keep a journal of the funny things your kids say and read it when you need a good laugh. The laughter will help relieve some of the effects of stress and worry.

5—"Run Away" From Worry: Ask yourself, "How can I move my body today?"

I've heard it said that food is the most overused anxiety drug and exercise is the most underused antidepressant. How is exercise an antidepressant? Exercise causes your brain to produce increased levels of serotonin. This particular type of brain chemical (called a neurotransmitter) can make you feel euphoric and peaceful. It can also help reduce depression. After you exercise, you've got all this feel-good serotonin flowing through you; that's why you feel so good mentally after a workout! And on top of that, exercise decreases your body's cortisol levels. This means exercise not only helps reduce depression, but it also helps you to reduce the stress hormone that contributes to a build-up of fatty tissue and therefore weight gain.

If that's not enough, exercise has also been known to boost body image, increase self-confidence, and generate a sense of accomplishment. How's that for literally running away from stress and worry?

Could you see yourself fitting some form of exercise into your daily activities? Could you take the kids out for afternoon walks? Could you have daily dance-offs with the littles in your family room? Could you ask your partner to watch the kids while you take a fitness class or pump some iron? Moving your body is one of the best things you can do to feel better now. Determine what kind of exercise you can fit into your life. When you do—aim for progress, not perfection. Starting small is still starting.

6—Accomplish One Small Task: Ask yourself, "Have I made my bed today?"

I read this great little book in May 2020 (eight weeks into the COVID-19 pandemic lockdown). The book is *Make Your Bed: Little Things That Can Change Your Life . . . and Maybe the World* by Admiral William H. McRaven. In it, he writes:

Every morning in basic SEAL training, my instructors, who at the same time were all Vietnam veterans, would show up in my barracks room, and the first thing they would inspect was your bed. If you did it right, the corners would be square, the covers pulled tight, the pillow centered just under the headboard and the extra blanket folded neatly at the foot of the rack.

It was a simple task, mundane at best. But every morning we were required to make our bed to perfection. It seemed a little ridiculous at the time, particularly in light of the fact that we were aspiring to be real warriors, tough battle-hardened SEALs, but the wisdom of this simple act has been proven to me many times over.

If you make your bed every morning, you will have accomplished the first task of the day. It will give you a small sense of pride and it will encourage you to do another task and another and another. By the end of the day, that one task completed will have turned into many tasks completed. Making your bed will also reinforce the fact that little things in life matter.

If you can't do the little things right, you will never do the big things right. And, if by chance you have a miserable day, you will come home to a bed that is made—that you made—and a made bed gives you encouragement that tomorrow will be better.

If you want to change the world, start off by making your bed.[12]

Mama Bear, the little action of making your bed can make a big difference in how you feel. Making progress makes you feel good. However, it's important to remember you're not a SEAL. This means there's no need for you to make your bed *perfectly*. But still, go ahead and make your bed. Then when you feel stressed, you can rest your head on a pillow in a bed that *you* made.

7—Develop Your Spiritual Life: Ask yourself, "What is one worry I will pray about today?"

Can we talk about the science of prayer for a second? In *Who Switched Off My Brain?: Controlling Toxic Thoughts and Emotions,* Dr. Caroline Leaf writes, "A growing body of scientific research confirms that prayer and actively developing your spiritual life increases frontal lobe activity, thickness, intelligence, and overall health."[13] Whoa, think about that for a minute!

How does prayer help in letting go of worry? The frontal lobe carries out higher mental processes. You use your frontal lobe to think, a pretty essential ingredient in challenging your assumptions *and* mastering your mind. You use your frontal lobe to make plans, like planning your actions to control the controllable. You use it to make decisions, such as what to do, what to read, who to ask, and what to think! In essence, your frontal lobe is used both to think and to decide what it is you will think about! And according to Dr. Leaf, praying helps strengthen your frontal lobe's ability to perform all those tasks. Therefore, scientifically speaking, engaging your spirit through prayer is a crucial component to transforming worried thinking into peace of mind.

You're a spiritual being. You are body, soul, and spirit. You have a spiritual nature that is separate and distinct both from your soul (made up of thoughts and emotions) and from the physical body in which you live. During those times in your life when you need some calm, some help with your difficulties, or some release from your burdens, consider incorporating prayer into your life.

Prayer is a critical human spiritual activity. Millions of people in all cultures, races, and religions pray. Here are three components of strategic prayer: ask, seek, and knock.

1. **Ask.** In other words, make a request. When you ask in prayer, you will receive an answer. I have discovered this to be true, time and time again, in my own

practice of prayer. Maybe you're saying, "I've asked! Why weren't my prayers answered?" I hear you. I've come to think of it like this: When people ask "Why weren't my prayers answered?" what they really mean is "Why didn't I specifically get what I prayed for?" It's important to understand that when I say your prayers will be answered, I'm not saying you will always get what you're asking for—I'm saying you will get an answer. Sometimes the answer is "Yes." Sometimes the answer is "No." Sometimes the answer is "Not yet." Regardless of the answer, trust that your prayers are not being ignored. "Ask and [an answer] will be given to you" (Matt. 7:7, New International Version).

2. **Seek.** With strategic prayer, you must seek in order to find. In other words, actively keep your eyes and ears open for the answer. The response to your prayers may be found in what a person says to you or in what happens around you. It may come in the form of something you observe or even in something you read. "Seek and you will find" (Matt. 7:7, NIV).

3. **Knock.** Knocking means taking action. It means you have prayerfully asked and identified guidance you've received on what your next steps could be, so now it's time to take those steps. For example, maybe you've prayed for a job. (That's step one: ask.) Then someone tells you about a job opening at a company. You were listening, and that's why you heard about this opportunity. (That's step two: seek.) And then you don't do anything except keep praying for a job. Whoops! You missed the third step: knock—take action! You need to knock, and when the door is opened, you must take the steps to get through it. "Knock and the door will be opened to you" (Matt. 7:7, NIV).

Instead of worrying about your circumstances, you can take the action of praying about them. Ask—make a request. Seek—keep your eyes and ears open for the answer. Knock—take action when those next steps are revealed. A renewed mind includes renewed thinking. To feel better, we must think better. Engaging your spirit through strategic prayer is an important step to thinking better.

8—Boost Serotonin: Ask yourself, "Who will I extend kindness to today?"

I have always loved the quote "The world is full of good people. But if you can't find one, be one!" Acts of kindness—no matter how small they may seem—can ripple out and impact the world in profound ways. They can also impact your health in a very positive way.

Acts of kindness are also a way to cause your brain to increase serotonin levels. This increase in the production of serotonin occurs when you observe, receive, or extend an act of kindness. We can't always catch an act of kindness "in the act," and we can't control when others are kind to us. However, we can control when we extend acts of kindness and connection to others.

This means you have the power to boost your mood anytime you choose by simply being kind. For instance, the same heady highs you get from receiving a real card in the mail—with an actual stamp on it—can be yours by sending someone else a real card in the mail! It's like a pyramid scheme, but for brain chemicals!

The next time you're feeling worried, shift your thinking away from your worried thoughts and onto ways to be kind to others in your life.

Take a Break—Share Kindness

Here's an idea that incorporates the kindness strategy. Choose someone you know and send them a note of thanks or encouragement.

Dear [**name of recipient**],

This note is to let you know I appreciate you.

Thank you for being the best [**kid/partner/friend/ employee/boss**] *I could hope for!*

It means so much to me when you [**laugh at my jokes—even when they're not so funny/help me back up when I stumble/make sure I'm getting enough riboflavin**].

Your [**encouraging words/hugs/morning texts**] *make such a huge difference! I want you to know that you matter, and I am extremely thankful for you.*

Love, [**your name**]

Sending this note to someone today is going to make both of you feel oh so good! Those wonderful feelings will go a long way in helping you let go of worry. Wait! I think I can hear the serotonin flowing already.

9—Overcome "Request for Help" Triggers: Ask yourself, "What do I need help with today? Who could I ask to help me?"

Why is the idea of asking for help so triggering? Sometimes we don't ask for the help we need because we have a hard time giving up control. Sometimes we feel upset because we think our partners should know what we need without us having to spell it out. At other times it's a matter of self-worth. Let's address these triggers now.

First, recognize that sometimes if you want a thing done *at all*, you have to let someone else do it. Second, your partner is not a mind reader, so be specific and straightforward with requests. Third, you are worthy. You are good enough. And you can ask for help. Lastly, if you're parenting solo, do you have a friend or relative who could help you? Or do you know any other single parents who would be open to brainstorming ideas for you both to help each other? We need each other. Be willing to accept—and to give—help. If guilt pops up when you realize you need some help, you can kick that guilt to the curb. Guilt is like the guest who stays at your party too long. Grab its coat, call it an Uber, and get it out of your house. (For hints on how to let go of guilt, check out Chapter 13.)

> Guilt is like the guest who stays at your party too long. Grab its coat, call it an Uber, and get it out of your house.

10—Practice Gratitude: Ask yourself, "What three things am I thankful for today? What made today great?"

"Are we almost there yet?" asked my three-year-old daughter Lindsay, only fifteen minutes into a two-hour family road trip.

"Not yet," I said.

After she asked the same question far too many times for my liking, I said, "Lindsay, we're not almost there yet. Please stop asking that question."

She agreed to stop asking. Then, five minutes later, she said, "I all-of-a-sudden realized we aren't almost there yet. Are we?"

Her dad and I laughed so hard. This little girl had figured out that by rearranging her words she could stick to her promise to not ask us "Are we there yet?"

The laughter relieved my frustration, so I could calmly say, "We're not almost there yet. You don't have to ask anymore because we'll tell you when we're almost there. Okay?"

"Okay," Lindsay agreed. Ninety seconds later, her little voice from the back seat asked, "Are you almost going to tell me that thing yet?"

That is one smart kid!

Are your little ones the same way on a long trip? Do they continue to ask you "Are we there yet?" Can you remember the impatience *you* felt as a kid during long trips? Now that you're all grown up, the question is this: Are you still impatient on the journey?

I have heard it said that the shortest period of time in North America is the time between when the light turns green and when you hear the first horn honk. What's the rush? We are both in the turning lane to take our minivans to Walmart. I doubt either of us has to go defuse a bomb while picking up matching pajamas for the family.

Many of us have carried this "destination impatience" into adulthood. When we have babies, we can't wait for them to get older so they will sleep through the night. When they get older, we can't wait for them to go to school. When they go to school, we can't wait for them to graduate. When they graduate, we can't wait until they move out. When they move out, we can't wait until they come back! Sound familiar?

We feel impatient because we convince ourselves that once we reach the next destination, we'll finally be content. The trouble is, once we arrive at that next destination, we may not be satisfied with where we are because we haven't learned to be truly grateful for what we have. In addition to our dissatisfaction, we may also feel remorse about the things we miss from the past.

All of this dissatisfaction and remorse troubles our hearts. It causes us to worry and feel anxious. The remedy for destination impatience is to be thankful in the moment. Be thankful now. In the middle of the crisis. In the middle of the stress. Be thankful on the journey, not just at the destination.

To be thankful on the journey, it helps to differentiate between the words "in" and "for." There's a big difference between the two. You don't have to be thankful *for* what's happening to be thankful *in* what's happening.

That means you don't have to wait until your kids are older, your finances have improved, or your job is secure. You can have peace in the middle of it all by setting your dial to gratitude.

You'll find the most successful people are the most thankful people, and the most thankful people are the happiest people. To create more joy and reduce stress, focus on the abundance you already possess.

Consider starting a gratitude challenge in your family. Who will you enlist to practice gratitude with you? Will you have your kids play along? Challenge each other with these two daily questions: "What three things am I thankful for today? What made today great?"

11—Simplify Your Life: Ask yourself, "What on my to-do list can I let go of today?

Take a really good look at your daily routine and see where you can simplify. Perhaps for you, that means setting specific morning and afternoon routines, or maybe delegating chores to family members. The solutions will be unique for each family. The ultimate goal here is to simplify things as much as possible. That includes knowing which tasks to take off your to-do list. The thing that will stretch you to your maximum tension point faster than you can say "snap" is the belief that you have to do it all. To erase and replace that self-limiting belief, think of it this way: Success is not achieved by doing everything. Success is achieved by doing what needs to be done and knowing what to leave undone.

If you're at your snapping point, look at your to-do list and ask yourself, "What are the most important things on this list for me to do? What things can I leave undone? What tasks can I delegate to someone else?"

12—Manage Your Commitments: Ask yourself, "Would I benefit physically, emotionally, or mentally from saying no to some requests today?"

Are you taking on too much because you're afraid of losing approval if you say no to someone else? A major key in reducing stress is learning to manage your commitments. Jim Rohn, author and success expert, said it best: "Learn how to say no. Don't let your mouth overload your back."[14] If you struggle with people-pleaser tendencies, here are three worry-free ways to say "no" nicely:

1. **Compliment and decline:** "Your book club sounds like fun. However, I'm not available to join."
2. **Thank and decline:** "I appreciate you thinking of me for this parent-volunteer opportunity. Regrettably, I'm unavailable to help this time."
3. **Give best wishes and decline:** "I wish you great success with your function. Unfortunately, I'm not available to participate this year."

Recognize that, in each example, you're not giving an explanation of *why* you're declining. You're simply declining. Nor are you closing the door on future requests. You're only saying, "Not this time." But know that this doesn't mean you must decline all requests. Getting together with friends and loved ones is important. Both accepting and giving help are beneficial to your well-being. Go ahead and make room to accept commitments when you can. At the same time, be mindful of your stress level. If you're nearing—or have already reached—your snapping point, avoid taking too much on for the sake of pleasing someone else.

There you have it: Twelve actions you can take to reduce the effects of worry. Now imagine you're holding that rubber band again. You have it stretched out to what seems to be its maximum tension point. This time though, instead of stretching it beyond the snap point, you begin to release the tension. What happens to the rubber band? It goes back to its original relaxed state—and just like that rubber band, you can too!

Take a Break—Self-Care Bingo

It's time for Self-Care Bingo! For four weeks, starting today, each time you complete one of the self-care strategies on the bingo card on the following page, highlight it! Your goal is to get at least one Bingo over the next four weeks. To get a Bingo, you need to highlight five horizontal, five vertical, five diagonal, or four corner squares. You can start right now by highlighting the free space in the center of the card—and, of course, the square in the bottom right-hand corner! You can use this bingo card or create your very own using your favorite self-care strategies. Using some colorful blotters and screaming "BINGO!" is entirely optional.

Reached my water goal for the day	Extended kindness to another	Hugged someone I love	Made time to pray	Moved my body
Took some deep calming breaths	Took time to enjoy a cup of tea	Listed three things I'm thankful for	Spent time talking with a friend	Had a bath/bubble bath/shower
Spent fifteen minutes outside	Went for a walk	FREE	Fed my body nutritious food	Made my bed
Made progress toward my meaningful goal	Listened to uplifting or energizing music	Removed something from my to-do list	Got rid of three items of clutter	Treated myself to something that nurtured me
Created some quiet time	Asked for help	Rested when I could	Had a good laugh	Read a page in my book

CHAPTER 10

Execute Bold Action

How to Make Value-Based Decisions and Take Courageous Action

One day, I was on the phone with my dad, and he said something that shocked me: "I was always jealous of your grandfather when you kids were little because he could always tell you girls he loved you, and you two would crawl all over him."

My dad and I didn't have a close relationship, and that was one of the most vulnerable things he'd ever said to me. At the time of that call, I was an adult with two daughters of my own, and up until that point in my life, I'd never believed my dad loved me.

That was a painful belief growing up. I tried so hard to be worthy and deserving of my dad's love, but it was a struggle, and no matter how hard I tried, I didn't feel loved. I felt rejected.

During this call with my dad, I didn't ask him any follow-up questions. But once we hung up, I couldn't stop thinking about what he had said. *If my dad was jealous of my grandfather because he could tell me he loved me, maybe that means my dad loves me.* I wanted to call him back right away and ask him what he had meant by those words, but I was afraid. *What if I ask him and I don't get the answer I so desperately want to hear? What if I take the risk and he rejects me?*

It took me about a week to muster up enough courage to call him back. In a moment of strength and determination, I dialed my dad's number. His phone was ringing. My heart was pounding. *I can't do this. I'll talk about the weather. I'll tell a joke.* I was beginning to chicken out and plot my escape from having an honest, meaningful conversation.

"Hello?" my dad said into the phone.

Oh no! He answered! It's okay, I can do this.

"Hi, Dad." As soon as those first two words left my mouth, I began to cry. Through my sobs, I said, "I want to thank you for having the courage to tell me you were jealous of Grandad because it made me think that you love me, and all my life, I never thought you did."

My dad replied, "Denise, I really, *really* love you."

I felt it. For the first time in my life, I felt loved by my dad. It was like this little five-year-old girl inside me came to life and started jumping for joy. *My dad loves me!* I felt happy and free. I had taken bold action, and it freed me.

Can you relate? Is there a bold action you've been putting off or avoiding because it feels too scary or too difficult to do? Have you ever mustered up enough courage to take that bold action and, like me, discovered it ended up setting you free?

Fear and worry can make you freeze. Bold action conquers fear. Bold action makes you free.

What Is Bold Action?

Bold action is different than ordinary action. For example, brushing your teeth, eating breakfast, and buying groceries are—for most people—ordinary actions. They're important to do but they're things you already do, and you can do them without much thought or effort. Bold actions, on the other hand, are actions that require courage or strength to take.

Here are some examples: Suppose you value family, but you've had an argument with a relative, and now you're worried you've offended that person. A bold action to take could be calling that family member to apologize, ask for forgiveness, and find resolution. That takes courage. It's bold!

Suppose you value health and fitness, and you've been wanting to join a gym but have let fear and insecurity stop you. A bold action for you could be signing up and attending that first class. Or maybe you need help to regain control over alcohol consumption; in that case, you could reach out to a twelve-step program. That is most certainly a courageous act. For me, calling my dad for an honest conversation about his comment was a bold action. It took courage to act in the face of fear. While bold actions can be scary to take, they often have the greatest impact on your life.

> Executing bold action is about making value-based decisions and taking courageous steps forward on those values.

Boldness is a leadership trait, and Mama Bear, you are a leader. You lead your child every day. You lead by example through the parenting choices you make and the way you love your family, yourself, and others. So as a leader in your family, what does it mean for you to *execute bold action*?

Executing bold action is about making value-based decisions and taking courageous steps forward on those values.

Identify Your Values

First, you must identify your values. Simply put, your values are your guiding principles for living a good life. Knowing your values can ease the overwhelm of parenting decisions, personal decisions, and even big life-altering decisions. Your values act as a compass, quickly directing you to conclusions with less stress and worry.

Suppose, for instance, you have the choice of staying in your marriage or giving up on it. Being crystal clear on what your values are can help you to decide which direction to take. If you value a two-parent family for your kids, and the main reason you want out of your marriage is that you think the grass is greener on the other side, remaining strong in your values can help you make the hard choice of doing what it takes to work on your marriage. That's called making value-based decisions. (Please note, however, that if you're in an abusive relationship, put down this book and take the bold action of getting help.)

It wasn't until 2017, when I became strong in my faith, that I even gave much thought to my own personal values. I'd heard it said: "If you don't stand for something, you'll fall for anything." I fell for a lot of "anythings" in my life that didn't end up being so good for me. Today, before taking bold action, I check in with my values and beliefs. If the action is not in alignment with my values and beliefs, I know it's not an action that's in my best interest to take.

Have you ever sat down and really considered your values? The following list contains fifty examples. Read over the list and select your top ten values. From that list of ten, try to narrow it down to your top three. These aren't the only values you may have, but they are a good starting point. (See the notes at the back of this book for a printable list of nearly four hundred values, available on my website.)[15]

Adventure	Fun	Parenting
Beauty	Generosity	Perseverance
Benevolence	Happiness	Positive attitude
Calmness	Harmony	Punctuality
Children	Health and fitness	Relationships
Cleanliness	Helpfulness	Respect
Compassion	Honesty	Responsibility
Connection	Humor	Spirituality
Cooperation	Imagination	Sharing
Courage	Independence	Solitude
Education	Inquisitiveness	Teamwork
Encouragement	Joy	Thoughtfulness
Fairness	Kindness	Tidiness
Faith	Leadership	Tolerance
Family	Making a difference	Trust
Financial security	Open-mindedness	Unity
Freedom	Nature	

Think of the top three values you selected as your *core* values. Maybe, like for me, family is in your top three core values. Maybe what gives you the greatest joy is making a difference. Perhaps you believe that honesty is the best policy and of utmost importance in your life. There are many types of values. Selecting your top three core values will help you to make decisions with greater ease and to stay focused on what matters most to you. Here are some questions you can ask yourself to help you determine your core values:

1. **What gives my life meaning and purpose?**
2. **What is important to me?**
3. **What brings me the most joy?**

While you're taking the time to ponder the answers to those questions, be aware that your first answers might be based on someone else's opinion. Society regularly tells us we should want certain things, like a certain type of body shape, or a certain level of education, or a certain type of house. Don't let other people's opinions dictate your answers. When you strive to become who or what you think others want you to become, it will leave you feeling unfulfilled.

You were created perfectly for a purpose. Take time to reflect on your own values. Let your answers be based on what *truly* matters to you. Once you've identified your values, you're in a good position to make value-based decisions. If you're still sitting on the fence about whether to take action or not, try this decision-making tool.

Check Your Decisions against Your Values

The following chart is a decision-making tool to help you sort through your thoughts and determine which actions are right for you based on your values. Be mindful that you still need to use your best discretion and wisdom before taking action on a major decision. However, this is a good starting place to help you problem solve and sort your way through the decision-making process.

First, ask yourself, "Is this decision in alignment with my values?" Then circle the YES at the top of the chart or the NO at the bottom of the chart.

Second, ask yourself, "Is this decision fear-driven?" "Fear-driven" means you're making your choice out of fear. For instance, purchasing a house you don't really like—because you're afraid you'll never get into the housing market if you don't act right now—is a fear-driven decision. So is choosing to say nothing while your in-laws violate your boundaries because you're worried about what they will think about you if you stand up for yourself and your children. Saying you'll attend a night out even when you're exhausted because you're afraid of missing out is fear-driven.

It's important to note that just because an action *feels* scary to take doesn't mean it's a fear-driven decision. For instance, purchasing your first home can feel scary. However, deciding to go ahead with the purchase because you've found a house that is right for your family and fits well with your financial situation is not a fear-driven decision; it is a hope-driven decision. You're hoping to build a home for your family, and you've chosen one after carefully considering your needs. Choosing to talk to your in-laws (or others) about your boundaries can *feel* scary, but it's definitely not a fear-driven decision. It's hope-driven because you're hoping to maintain healthy boundaries and harmony within your family. Taking action on hope-driven decisions requires courage, but it also tends to have the greatest positive impact on our lives.

So let's get back to that question: Is the decision you're making fear-driven? Circle the YES at the left of the chart or the NO at the bottom of the chart.

	Is this decision in alignment with my values? YES		
Is this decision fear-driven? YES	YELLOW LIGHT	GREEN LIGHT	Is this decision fear-driven? NO
	RED LIGHT	RED LIGHT	
	NO Is this decision in alignment with my values?		

Finally, connect the dots. Draw a line from the answer you circled at the top or bottom of the chart to the answer you circled on the left or right of the chart. The line you drew to connect your answers will intersect in the middle. It will cut across the words "GREEN LIGHT," "RED LIGHT," or "YELLOW LIGHT."

Green light means go! Your decision is in alignment with your values, and your decision is not fear-driven. This is a good indication you've got an action worth taking on your hands.

Red light means stop. Whether your decision is fear-driven or not, you've decided it's not in alignment with your values. It isn't wise to make a move that goes against your values, comprises your integrity, or disregards your beliefs. It's like sailing through a red light with your kids in the car and getting caught by a red-light camera. This isn't the "family snapshot" you want in your home!

Yellow light means more information is required. Use the tools you've learned so far in this book. Ask yourself, "What am I afraid of? What assumptions am I making? Is what I'm thinking true, fact, or helpful? Who could I ask? What could I do? What could I read?" Examine your thoughts and feelings further so you can uncover the fear before leaping into something you could later regret.

When fear, doubt, and worry are attempting to stop you from following through on your action plan, build your confidence by checking in with your values to see whether the action is worth taking. If you've decided that it is, you can more confidently move forward even in the presence of fear. Just like I discovered when I took the bold action of calling my dad, fear makes you freeze, but bold action sets you free.

I want to add a special note here on being bold: What matters is that you do your best. On some days, your best will be different than on other days. When you're going through a crisis, when getting through the end of the day takes strength and courage, doing so is both bold enough and a job well done!

Mama Bear, what are your values? Is there a bold action you've been putting off or avoiding because it feels too scary or too difficult to do? Is that bold action in alignment with your values? Only you can decide what is right for you. However, if you decide this particular bold action is right for you, I encourage you to take action today because of what you will become: a more fulfilled, more courageous, happier you!

In this step of the CALM process, you've learned how to craft an action plan by asking yourself, "Who could I ask? What could I do? What could I read?" You've learned how to overcome some of the fears and roadblocks that prevent people from following through on their action plans. You've read about specific actions you can take to reduce the physical and emotional effects of stress and worry. You've discovered how to execute bold action by making value-based decisions and taking courageous action on those things that matter most to you.

Of course, you won't always be able to control what's happening around you. Fortunately, coming up in Part 3, you'll learn specific strategies to let go of the uncontrollable. In other words, you'll be equipped with the tools to stop worrying about things over which you have no control. In the meantime, continue to challenge your assumptions and take action to control the things you can.

Take a Break—Word Search

Hidden in the following puzzle are thirteen values. Can you find them?

E	G	N	I	R	A	H	S	H	N
E	R	X	A	U	Q	S	K	O	N
Y	A	U	N	T	E	Y	I	N	E
M	L	I	T	N	U	T	T	E	R
W	T	I	R	N	A	R	X	S	D
Y	F	I	M	C	E	J	E	T	L
R	A	U	U	A	O	V	D	Y	I
F	C	D	N	Y	F	M	D	O	H
R	E	S	P	E	C	T	N	A	C
B	V	S	S	E	N	D	N	I	K

Word List:

ADVENTURE	FUN	RESPECT
CHILDREN	HONESTY	SHARING
EDUCATION	JOY	UNITY
FAIRNESS	KINDNESS	
FAMILY	NATURE	

PART 3

Let Go of the Uncontrollable

When dealing with something beyond your control,
make letting go of it your goal.

Picture a drinking glass holding eight ounces of water. Imagine yourself picking it up to have a drink. Would it feel very heavy? Unless your arm is injured, it's not too heavy. Now imagine taking that glass of water in your hand and, this time, holding it out with your arm extended.

How do you think you would feel if you kept your arm extended and held the glass of water for several minutes? It's likely your arm and shoulder muscles would start to burn. The longer you held it, the heavier those eight ounces of water would feel! In the end, what matters most is not how much the glass of water weighs but how long you try to hold it.

Your burdens and worries can be like that glass of water: the longer you hold them, the heavier they can feel. When a worry pops up, determine whether it's productive or counterproductive. If it's productive—that is, if it's prompting you to do something—take action. If it's counterproductive—if you're worrying about something over which you have no control—then let it go.

Sometimes letting go can feel very difficult—especially when you feel like your concerns are justified—but that's what this next step in the CALM process, the letter L, will help you to accomplish: Let Go of the Uncontrollable. Here you'll learn strategies to stop worrying about those things beyond your control and free yourself from the burden of carrying that mental and emotional load.

To begin with, here's a poem that has given me clarity and peace about letting go of two very specific things: the problems of yesterday and the burdens of tomorrow.

Yesterday, Today, and Tomorrow
Author Unknown

There are two days in every week
about which we should not worry,
Two days which should be kept free of fear and apprehension.

One of these days is YESTERDAY,
With its mistakes and cares,

Its faults and blunders,
Its aches and pains.
YESTERDAY has passed forever beyond our control.

All the money in the world cannot bring back YESTERDAY.
We cannot undo a single act we performed;
We cannot erase a single word we said.
YESTERDAY is gone.

The other day we should not worry about is TOMORROW
With its possible adversities, its burdens, its larger promise.
TOMORROW is also beyond our immediate control.

TOMORROW, the sun will rise,
Either in splendor or behind a mask of clouds,
But it will rise.
Until it does, we have no stake in TOMORROW
For it is as yet unborn.

This leaves only one day—TODAY.
Anyone can fight the battles of just one day.
It is only when you and I add the burdens of those two awful
    eternities—
YESTERDAY and TOMORROW—
That we break down.

It is not the experience of TODAY that drives people mad.
It is remorse or bitterness for something which happened
YESTERDAY
And the dread of what TOMORROW may bring.

Let us, therefore, live but ONE day at a time.[16]

In the upcoming chapters, you'll learn strategies to stop worrying about those two uncontrollable days—yesterday and tomorrow. You'll also learn how to stop worrying about those uncontrollable things you're dealing with in the present by learning how to let go of upset feelings, forgive others and yourself, free yourself from guilt, let go of judgment, reduce perfectionism, and choose faith over fear.

CHAPTER 11

Let Go of Upset Feelings

The "Stinkin' Thinkin'" Edition

A wise mom once sat in a large group of people and told an exceptionally funny joke. Everyone laughed whole-heartedly. A minute or so passed, and then the wise mom repeated the joke. This time, fewer people laughed. The wise mom continued to tell the same joke over and over until there was ab-solutely no laughter in response. Then the wise mom smiled and asked, "Why is it you don't laugh at the same joke again and again, yet you keep crying over the same thing again and again?"

Are you telling yourself a story over and over that makes you feel sad, stuck, worried, or afraid? The good news is, by using the strategies in this chapter, you can learn how to let go of upset feelings, release regret, and stop fretting about things over which you have no control.

Here are some examples of things beyond your control that can make you feel upset and possibly even sorry for yourself:

¤ You looked forward to your family vacation all year, but the kids argued the entire time.

¤ You didn't plan on becoming a single parent, but now you are one.

¤ You stood by your bestie when she needed you, and now when you need her the most, she's not here for you.

Life has many unexpected twists and turns. When circumstances or people fall short of your expectations, it's very easy to feel upset, angry, hurt, and frustrated. Is it wrong for you to feel the way you feel when things don't turn out as you'd hoped? Of course not. Your feelings are valid. And acknowledging that fact is the first step to moving on.

Validate Your Feelings

It's important for you to validate your feelings. That means you acknowledge how you're feeling and reassure yourself that it's okay to feel the way you do. Validating your feelings helps you to trust your own wants and needs. It helps you to make good life choices and set healthy boundaries.

If you have a hard time accepting that it's okay for you to feel the way you do, it could be that you weren't raised in a validating environment. Here's an example:

Imagine you're a child and your dog dies. Your parent sees you crying. In a validating environment, your parent would comfort you and say, "Of course

> Validating your feelings helps you to trust your own wants and needs. It helps you to make good life choices and set healthy boundaries.

you're sad. You loved your dog very much." The message you would receive is that your emotions and feelings are correct, that it's okay for you to feel sad.

In an invalidating environment, your parent would see you crying and say, "Stop crying. It's just a dog. We can get another one." The message you would receive then is that that you shouldn't be feeling the way you do, that you're wrong for feeling sad.

Adults who were raised in environments where their feelings were not validated may have trouble making decisions, asking for and accepting help, and tending to their own wants and needs. As an adult, you may often make yourself "wrong" for feeling the way you do, and you can get stuck in life as a result. It's hard to make choices and move forward when you don't believe that your feelings are valid. Even when you have an overwhelming sense that you're not where you want to be in your life, or that your needs are not being met, you may stop yourself from doing anything about it.

Right now, you might be thinking, *This makes so much sense. I wasn't raised in a validating home. It's all my parents' fault that I've been feeling the way I do!* That's a great realization, but remember, this isn't about negatively judging your parents for the part they played in your past. We're all doing the best we can with the tools we have. Parents may unintentionally invalidate their child's feelings because they simply don't want to see their child upset. That's one reason why parents may see their child crying and say, "Don't be sad."

Mama Bear, it's not too late to start validating both your feelings and your children's feelings. Here's how:

- **Actively listen.** Listen to yourself by paying attention to how you're feeling, and listen to your children by allowing them to express their feelings to you without interruption.
- **Acknowledge feelings.** You can acknowledge your feelings and your children's feelings by saying, "It makes sense that you're feeling the way you do."

¤ **Offer reassurance.** Reassure yourself and your children by saying, "It's okay for you to feel the way you do."

There are long-term benefits to validating your children's feelings. It helps them learn to trust their needs and wants, strengthens their ability to express their emotions, and gives them the self-confidence to make healthy choices . . . even into adulthood. Go ahead, Mama Bear—validate your child's feelings and validate your own. Feel all the feels and be assured that it's okay for you to feel the way you do. Just like validating your children's feelings gives them the self-confidence to make healthy choices, it does the same for you. This includes making the healthy choice to let go of upset feelings, like you're learning to do here.

Identify Cognitive Distortions

Once you've validated your feelings, check in with the story you're telling yourself. Better yet, grab a journal and write down everything that's upsetting you about your current situation or past experience. Be as detailed as you can. Get every upsetting part of your story out of your heart and mind onto paper and into the open.

Have you done it? Once you've finished, examine your story for cognitive distortions. A cognitive distortion is an automatic way of looking at situations without examining other—more accurate—possibilities.

Famous motivational speaker Zig Ziglar once said, "We all need a daily check up from the neck up to avoid stinkin' thinkin' which ultimately leads to hardening of the attitudes."[17] In Chapter 17, you'll learn how to gain a winning attitude that sets you up for success. In the meantime, let's continue to examine your upsetting story for any cognitive distortions.

The following list contains examples of stinkin' thinkin'—cognitive distortions that can fuel all kinds of upset feelings, including worry, anger, sadness, self-pity, and regret. Take a look at the list to see if any of these distortions are playing a leading role in the story you've been telling yourself. If they are, you can use the remedies listed to help revise that story into a more accurate—and more positive—narrative.

Stinkin' Thinkin': Types and Remedies

Type	Definition	Remedy
All-or-nothing amplifying	Thinking in extremes, often using absolutes such as "never," "always," "everything," or "nothing."	Replace all-or-nothing statements with more accurate terms, such as "rarely," "often," "once in a while," or "some things."
Assuming	Accepting something as true—or as certain to happen—without proof.	Challenge your assumptions (see Part 1).
Catastrophizing	Believing that a situation is far worse than it actually is and that you won't be able to handle the outcome.	Talk to someone else to get another viewpoint. Focus on actions you can take to control the controllable, and then let go of the uncontrollable. Affirm your abilities by saying to yourself, "I can handle it."
Discounting positives	Rejecting the positives, believing they are unimportant or untrue.	Allow positives to come into your mind and heart. For instance, when you receive a compliment, say thank you rather than dismissing it.
Making feelings facts	Believing without further investigation that your feelings are facts and therefore always tell you the truth.	Validate your feelings, but also search to uncover the root belief that might be creating the upsetting emotions. Remember, your feelings are not always telling you the truth.

Positive–blocking	Choosing to only see what's wrong instead of what's right.	Shift your attention to what is going well. Consider what you have left instead of only what you have lost. Consider what you're thankful for instead of what you feel you're lacking.
Should–ing	Examining situations and people based on how you think they should be, rather than how they actually are.	Accept "what is" (see Chapter 15). Life is never going to be perfect. By all means, take action to control the things you can and then let go of the things you can't by accepting "what is."

Flip the Script

Mama Bear, are you able to spot any types of stinkin' thinkin' in the upsetting story you've been telling yourself? If you do, congratulations, you're human! Identifying these cognitive distortions in your thinking will help you flip the script.

Flipping the script is about telling yourself a new story with a more positive narrative. It involves recognizing and replacing any cognitive distortions using the remedies provided.

Let's use one of the scenarios listed at the beginning of this chapter to illustrate what flipping the script looks like in practice: You've been looking forward to your family vacation all year, but the kids argued the entire time. It's easy to see how dwelling on this narrative can lead to upset feelings long after the arguing—and the vacation—have ended.

A great way to help you flip the script here is to use the remedies for all-or-nothing amplifying and positive-blocking. Let's start with all-or-nothing amplifying. The remedy for this distortion is to replace all-or-nothing statements with more accurate terms to describe what happened. Is it really true that the kids argued "the entire time"? Or would it be more accurate to say they argued "often" or even "once in a while"?

Next, try the remedy for positive-blocking. Remember, positive-blocking is about choosing to see only what's wrong instead of what's right. Putting the kids' behavior to the side for a moment, what was the very best part of the trip for you? Look for the positives: What parts of the vacation are you thankful for? Was there a moment during the trip that filled your heart with gratitude?

The more you focus on what went right, the better you'll begin to feel. Using more accurate truths can help you finally leave those upset feelings about past events and experiences behind. By changing the stories you tell yourself, you'll become free from the emotional pain those old stories have been causing you. Upsetting, confusing, and unfair things happen in life. When they do, by all means validate your feelings, but also recognize and replace any stinkin' thinkin', take action to control the things you can, and then choose to let go and move forward.

Take a Break—Spot the Stinkin' Thinkin'

Your mission, should you choose to accept it, is to read the following scenario and then answer the skill-testing questions that follow. Here we go:

Scenario: I was always there for my best friend when she was going through a difficult time with her child, but now, when I need her the most, she is never there for me. My feelings are so hurt. Am I not worthy of her time?

Questions:

1. Are this Mama Bear's feelings valid?   Yes/No
2. Are there any cognitive distortions in Mama Bear's thinking?   Yes/No
3. Are there actions Mama Bear can take to control the controllable?   Yes/No

Answers:

Did you answer "Yes" to all three questions? Ding ding ding! We have a winner!

First, you're darn tootin' this Mama Bear's feelings are valid! It hurts when a friend pulls away from you. It's confusing when you don't understand why it's happening.

Next, what cognitive distortions did you spot? Did you catch the all-or-nothing words? Mama Bear used the words "always" and "never." The remedy listed for all-or-nothing amplifying suggests replacing all-or-nothing words like "always" and "never" with words like "often" and "rarely."

This Mama Bear could flip the script by changing her story. "I was **often** there for my best friend when she was going through a difficult time with her child," she could say, "and now when I need her the most, she is **rarely** there for me." This new story would help her regulate her emotions.

In addition, these kinds of words can be more accurate to the situation.

Did you also spot the hidden assumption in her statement? The hidden assumption here is that her friend is not responding because Mama Bear isn't worthy of her time. The remedy for assuming is to challenge your assumptions. Mama Bear could challenge her assumptions using any of the strategies we covered in Part 1, but let's use the strategy of rewriting the story.

Instead of assuming her friend doesn't care, Mama Bear could ask herself, "What else could it be?" It could be that Mama Bear's friend is overwhelmed by Mama Bear's emotions. Some people aren't equipped to handle the emotions of others and can become unresponsive to calls for help as a result.

Finally, are there actions this Mama Bear can take to control the controllable? Let's see: Can she control her friend's behavior? Nope. But Mama Bear might choose to take the action of phoning her friend and honestly expressing how she feels. This may influence her friend's behavior and strengthen their relationship. As we know, though, we can't control other people; the friend might not answer her call.

Where would this leave Mama Bear? Well, she could use the remedy for positive-blocking and consider what she has left (such as other family members and friends, her health, and her child) instead of focusing only on what she has lost (a friend). This doesn't mean Mama Bear can't still feel sad about the friendship. Again, her feelings are valid. But this remedy would help Mama Bear refocus on the positives and find comfort in family and friends who are there for her and who are happy for the opportunity to be a part of her life.

You Got This, Mama Bear!

Remember, you can let go of upset feelings. Try using these prompts:

1. **Validate your feelings:** Ask, "What am I feeling right now?" Then say, "It's okay for me to feel the way I feel."
2. **Identify cognitive distortions:** Ask, "What story am I telling myself about what happened? Am I all-or-nothing amplifying, assuming, catastrophizing, discounting positives, making feelings facts, positive-blocking, or shoulding?" If you can answer yes to any of these, move to the next step.
3. **Flip the script:** Replace your cognitive distortions with more accurate thoughts using the remedies provided in the Stinkin' Thinkin' list.

What is here for you today and what lies ahead for you in the future is far more important than what is already behind you. Keep pressing forward. Flip the script—it's time for a new story! Take action to control the things you can, and then choose to let go and move forward.

CHAPTER 12

Let Go through Forgiveness

The "Hurts and Offenses" Edition

I was around six years old when it happened. My aunt had been in an accident, and her thighs were severely burned. Our family had gone to visit with her while she was healing. I adored my aunt, and in my excitement to see her, I got too close and nudged her arm, which caused her cup of tea to spill onto her lap right where she had been burned.

My aunt screamed, and I jumped away, horrified. I was incredibly sorry that I had hurt her—I felt sick about what I had done—but I couldn't apologize, and the longer I went without apologizing, the more upset with me my mom became.

"Go and tell your Auntie that you're sorry," she kept saying. But I wouldn't do it. What I did do was walk back over to my aunt and give her my entire allowance. It wasn't a lot of money, but it was all I had, so it was a lot to me. However, my mom, as well as my other grown-up relatives, were still upset that I wouldn't say the words "I'm sorry."

Have you ever asked your children to do something only to have them stubbornly refuse? Perhaps if I explain why I wouldn't apologize then, it will help you to see that sometimes the reason for our children's behavior isn't simply because they are being difficult.

The reason I wouldn't apologize was that I thought you only apologized when you did something wrong *on purpose*. For instance, if I stuck my finger in the biggest chocolate pudding in the fridge to make sure it was the one I would get for dessert (and I did do that), I could apologize because it was wrong to do and I had done it on purpose. However, no matter how much I wanted to please my mom, I would not say I was sorry to my aunt because I didn't want her to think I had hurt her intentionally. So I refused to apologize.

Are you waiting for an apology that hasn't yet come? Are you waiting for others who have hurt you to say they're sorry before you're willing to let go of the resentment you feel? Unfortunately, for any of a variety of reasons, that apology may never come. It could be that the other person isn't aware they've hurt you. Maybe they don't know how to apologize. Maybe they don't care about what they've done. Whatever the reason, the good news is that you don't have to wait for an apology to begin letting go of the pain. You can let go through forgiveness.

Forgive to Help Yourself

It's tempting to hold on to the anger and bitterness you feel toward those who have hurt and offended you. You may feel that they don't deserve your forgiveness and that, by forgiving them, you're

Forgiveness doesn't let others off the hook for their wrongdoings; it lets you off the hook of resenting them for what's happened. It frees you from carrying that emotional pain.

letting them off the hook for all they have done. Forgiveness doesn't let others off the hook for their wrongdoings; it lets you off the hook of resenting them for what's happened. It frees you from carrying that emotional pain.

You see, being angry and bitter toward others doesn't change those other people. It changes you. It makes you miserable. Why not open the door to more peace and joy than you've ever known before by forgiving people who have hurt you in the past and choosing to be someone who is difficult to offend?

In our society, people are often too quick to close the door on relationships with friends and family over small offenses. I once heard a grown woman say, "I can't tell my sister I don't want to come for dinner next week. If I do that, she won't speak to me for years." Can you imagine living in that family? You'd be constantly walking on eggshells and neglecting your own needs and wants for fear of being cast out. Sadly, this happens in a lot of families, but it doesn't have to happen in yours. Instant rejection doesn't have to be the way you and your children respond to offenses.

Forgive to Help Your Children

You can become a role model of forgiveness for your child. When you model forgiveness for your children, not only are you teaching them how to treat others, but you're also teaching them how to treat you! Think about it this way: When you handle others' mistakes by turning your back on them—or even shutting them out of your life entirely—you are modeling for your kids how they should behave in the same situation. If they internalize that lesson, what do you think might happen when you make mistakes? Your children may do that very same thing to you and, someday, to their future children. And so the cycle perpetuates. However, when you model forgiveness and are a living example of someone who is difficult to offend, your children are much more likely to be forgiving toward you—even when they're all grown up.

If you are struggling with being this sort of positive role model, that is okay. You can start small. When someone cuts you off in traffic, instead of taking it personally, honking your horn, and saying things you'd rather not say in front of your kids, tell yourself, "I am difficult to offend. I am a forgiving person." Besides, why allow that individual to spoil your mood? You don't know what's happening in that person's life that caused them to cut you off like that. Could you choose to be difficult to offend? Could you forgive them and let it go so you can enjoy driving with your kids? I hope so, because it will make you feel so much better!

However, even when you're trying to be forgiving, there will be times when you have difficulty letting even small offenses go. Pay attention when this happens; it can be a reaction arising out of unresolved hurts from past grievances. When you're hurting inside, it will eventually come out somewhere. Your anger, upset, and frustration may be misdirected at people in your life who didn't cause the initial pain. You might blow up at your spouse for being a few minutes late. You might yell at your kids for not hanging up their jackets.

When this happens, explore your feelings. Look back at unresolved hurts from your past, and ask yourself the following questions. As these questions may take some reflection, you may even want to write your answers down. Ask yourself:

- **"Who do I need to forgive?"**
- **"What did that person do or say to me that was hurtful?"**
- **"How did that experience make me feel? What did it make me believe about myself?"**
- **"Is that belief true? If not, what is true?"**

Forgive to Unlearn Harmful Messages

You see, when something happens that hurts us, it makes us believe certain things about ourselves. We take these thoughts and beliefs into our hearts and minds. For instance, through painful experiences you've had throughout your life, you may have received messages like these: "I'm unloved." "I'm not safe." "I'm unwanted." "I'm broken."

Such messages are untrue. If you allow yourself to believe them, these messages can negatively affect every area of your life. Fortunately, these lies can be uncovered, and the wounds they created can be healed.

To show you how to use these questions to begin healing from past wounds and let go through forgiveness, here's an example from my own life:

"Who do I need to forgive?" My babysitter.

"What did that person do or say to me that was hurtful?" When I was eight years old, my babysitter locked me in my scary basement and turned out the lights. I was terrified of the basement as a kid. I had nightmares about it regularly—nightmares that usually involved a giant hand coming out of the basement to grab me from my bed. Being locked in the basement by the babysitter was like living out my worst dreams. I stood on the top step of the staircase, banging on the door, crying and begging for her to let me out. I'm not sure how long I was locked in there, but it felt like an eternity. When she finally let me out, she said, "You're such a big baby." Then she played with my older sister while I sat outside at our backyard picnic table, crying and feeling bad about myself for not being a more likeable person. I didn't tell my mom because I didn't want her to think I was a big baby too.

"How did that experience make me feel? What did it make me believe about myself?" I felt rejected, unliked, alone, and unsafe. I felt like it was my fault the babysitter had done this to me: I was unlikeable, a "big baby." The message implanted in my heart that day was that I was unwanted and unlovable and that it wasn't safe for me to be myself or to express my true feelings.

"Is that belief true?" No.

"If not, what is true?" The truth is that I have immense value and incredible worth—just like you do! I am wanted. I am lovable. I am safe to be myself and to express my true feelings. While my sense of self-worth felt diminished that day, my true worth cannot be altered by anyone or anything, and neither can yours.

"I can choose to forgive." I choose to forgive that babysitter for locking me in the basement. I release her from any apology or explanation I feel she owes me. I forgive myself for allowing her to have the power to define my self-worth. I take that power away from her now through forgiveness.

How about you? Who do you need to forgive? Is it yourself? Is it someone else? What happened? Did someone say or do something to you that was hurtful? How did it make you feel, and what did it make you believe about yourself? For instance, did what was said or done make you feel like you didn't matter, that you were all alone or not good enough, that you're damaged, that you're not safe, or that your life is completely ruined? Express your answers to those questions in writing.

Next, recognize any lies and reemphasize the truth to yourself. For example, did what was said or done make you believe you are flawed and have lost your worth? Is it true that you are flawed and have lost your worth? Absolutely not. Your *sense* of worth can be altered by believing lies that were planted in your heart. However, your *true* worth cannot be altered by anyone or anything. Regardless of what has or hasn't happened in your life, you have immense value and incredible worth. Receive that truth into your heart and mind!

Now, choose to forgive. In forgiving others, it's important to recognize you're not condoning poor behavior. You're simply understanding that you can't change what's happened, and you are choosing to forgive and move forward.

So that your new understanding becomes clear in your heart and mind, write out a forgiveness statement. If you're struggling with how to word it, try filling in the blanks of this example:

> *"I choose to forgive* **[the person's name]** *for* **[what was said or done]** *which made me feel* **[how you felt]** *and believe* **[what you believed]**. *I forgive myself for allowing* **[the person's name]** *to have the power to define my value, worth, or quality of life. I take that power away now through forgiveness."*

In this statement, you're forgiving yourself for allowing another person to have the power to define you. You're forgiving yourself for holding onto the anger and the bitterness from your experience. You're forgiving the other person for what happened and how they made you feel. You're taking back the power that was taken from you when you internalized the false messages their harmful acts taught you to believe about yourself. Finally, after you've written it all out, tear it up, rip it to shreds, and free yourself from it.

Forgive to Keep Moving Forward

You don't have to keep waiting for that apology before you can forgive—you don't even have to wait until you feel like forgiving to forgive—you can make that choice today. You can choose to forgive offenses that have taken place in the past *and* those that are taking place in the present.

Are you dealing with offenses in the present? Instead of internalizing it, dwelling on it, making assumptions about it, or taking it personally, declare, "I am difficult to offend. I am a forgiving person."

Dealing with offenses in the past? Ask yourself the questions listed above and write down your answers: "Who do I need to forgive? What did that person do or say to me that was hurtful? How did that experience make me feel? What did it make me believe about myself? Is that belief true? If not, what is true?" Rejecting the lies and receiving the truth allows hope to triumph over despair, faith over fear, and victory over defeat. Then choose to forgive. Just as you have forgiven others, forgive yourself too. There is grace and forgiveness available for you regardless of what has happened in your past. You can confidently declare, "I'm not going back. I'm moving ahead. My past is over. I'm forgiven, and I am forgiving."

Your past *is* over. By becoming a forgiving person, one who is difficult to offend, you'll be appreciative of the past, content with the present, and filled with hope for a bright future.

CHAPTER 13

Let Go of Guilt

The "Mom-Guilt" Edition

"**B**rianna, get out of my room," seven-year-old Lindsay begged her five-year-old sister. I could hear her upstairs even from where I was sitting in the living room. Obviously, Brianna wasn't listening to her request, because Lindsay's frustrated voice grew louder and louder. "Brianna, get *out* of my room! Brianna! Get. Out. Of. My. Room!"

As I listened, my heart started pounding. When Lindsay once again pleaded, "Get out of my room!" I realized I'd had all I could take. In the loudest mom-voice I could muster, I screamed, "Brianna, get out of Lindsay's rooooooooooooooooooooom!"

The emphasis I put on the word "room" is still etched in my memory. So is the sound of little Brianna jumping down off Lindsay's bed, running to her adjacent room, and closing the door: *Thump. Pitter-patter, pitter-patter, pitter-patter. Creak. Click.*

Silence.

Ugh! I felt terrible. I hadn't yelled at either of my kids like that before—and I haven't since. I went upstairs and apologized to Brianna right away.

I've heard it said, "Having one child makes you a parent. Having two kids makes you a referee." That day, I hadn't handled my role as referee well at all, and I felt very guilty about it.

Can you relate? Have you ever felt guilty about yelling at your kids? It's a common guilt trigger for moms.

Most of us have experienced mom-guilt at one time or another. It's that feeling that comes when you think you're not doing enough as a parent. It's that tied-up-in-knots feeling you get from making mistakes or believing that you're failing as a mom (even though you're doing your very best).

Mama Bear, you must do the work to release guilt so that those feelings don't turn into shame. You weren't meant to live your life pushed down by the weight of your past mistakes or perceived shortcomings. It's time to free yourself from the prison of guilt by unlearning patterns of self-judgment. The following six recommendations can help you move from feeling guilty to feeling guilt-free.

Eliminate the Word "Should"

One of the most highly loaded guilt-trigger words in our vocabulary is the word "should." Remember "should-ing" from the stinkin' thinkin' list in Chapter 11? Here's a quick reminder: should-ing is examining people and situations based on how you think they *should* be, rather than how they actually are.

For instance, many moms feel guilty if the house isn't as clean as they think it *should* be. Some moms feel guilty taking time out for self-care because they think they *should* be busy taking care of someone or something else. Some Mama Bears feel guilty about working outside of the home because they think they *should* be home with the kids. Others feel guilty for staying at home because they think they *should* be contributing to the family finances.

Take a moment to examine your own thoughts. Is the word "should" at the root of your guilty feelings? Are you thinking that things in your life *should* be different than they are and that you're the one to blame? Are you thinking *you* (or your children) should be different than the way you are and judging yourself harshly for it? If so, kick guilt to the curb by challenging your beliefs. Ask yourself, "Is it true? Is it fact? Is it helpful?"

Suppose you think you're a bad mom for feeling angry or impatient. Is it true? No. The truth is that good moms feel angry and impatient at times.

Suppose you think your mistakes are unforgivable and so you're a failure. Is it fact? Not a chance. The fact is that good moms make mistakes. You're worthy of forgiveness and grace. Mistakes are not failures, and you are not a failure for making them. You're a human being who is learning.

Suppose you think you're the only one struggling and that you should be able to manage everything like everyone else. Is it helpful? Nope. It's not helpful to beat yourself up over being human. How would that go, anyway? I can hear Joe Rogan saying, "Stepping into the UFC octagon, weighing none-of-your-business, is our imperfect mom! And running to the other corner of the ring is her opponent, weighing exactly the same—it's herself! She makes a left hook! She dodges! And . . . what's that? We have to reschedule the fight; she has to get dinner on the table."

Don't beat yourself up, Mama Bear. You're not the only one struggling. Good moms struggle. Just do your best!

Acknowledge That You're Doing Your Best

Doing your best doesn't mean doing it perfectly. Nobody's perfect, so don't demand perfection from yourself. You can only do your best. That's all any of us can do. Take it from Walt Disney: "Why worry? If you've done the very best you can, worrying won't make it any better."[18] And if you've done the very best you can, feeling guilty won't make it any better either. On some days your best will be different than on others. During times of heartbreak and loss, when you haven't had enough rest, when you're not feeling well physically, mentally, or emotionally, your best will be different than when you're feeling good. Do your best. Your best is enough, and *you* are enough—just as you are!

> We are all doing the best we can with the tools and knowledge we have in the moment. You're doing your best, and your best is enough.

Sometimes in order to see that you are enough, you need to adjust where you're focusing. You may see your mistakes, your stretch marks, your weight, your wrinkles, your age, the times you yelled when you thought you should have kept it together, the dishes piled in the sink, the baby food on your pajama bottoms, or the frozen pizza you feel guilty about putting into the oven for the kids' dinner, and then you might feel like you've failed. But guess what? Here's what I see, Mama Bear: I see the way you put your family first, the tantrums you tame, the sleepless nights, and the early-morning wake-ups. I see the countless meals you've prepared even when you weren't hungry yourself or you felt too tired to cook. Yet you pushed through, and you did it. Try to see yourself through my eyes.

Ask yourself, "Am I doing the best I can?" When answering that question, keep this in mind: We are all doing the best we can with the tools and knowledge we have in the moment. You're doing your best, and your best is enough.

Take Appropriate Action

So you've asked your child to pitch in with age-appropriate chores. "Why do I always have to do it?" your child whines in an attempt to get out of helping and get back to playing video games. "None of the other kids' moms make them do it."

Guilt starts to creep in. Halt it! Ask yourself, "Is what I'm doing appropriate in this situation?" Is it appropriate for you to ask your children to pitch in with age-appropriate chores and meal prep? Of course it is. In fact, it teaches them about responsibility and contributing to the family. Is it appropriate to take time out for self-care when you need it, even when there are dishes in the sink? It most certainly is! In fact, when you take time to address your needs, you'll discover you have more strength and patience than when you push yourself to exhaustion. Is it appropriate for you to cook a frozen pizza for dinner even though the Pinterest moms are cooking all-organic meals? Yes, it is, Mama Bear.

There's a popular quote online that says, "We would all love to be Pinterest Moms, but it's okay if you turn out to be more of an Amazon Prime Mom."[19] Comparison is the thief of joy. It's kind of like Robin Hood: stealing from the rich (in spirit) and giving to the poor (in attitude). It's time to call the cops on that thief! "Hello, police? Yes, it's me again. Comparison came into my house in broad daylight and stole my joy . . . Well, I disagree! I think it is an emergency."

There's no need for you to compare yourself to others. There's no need for you to compare yourself to the kind of mom you think you should be. You're the kind of mom your child needs just by being you.

Sometimes simply acknowledging to yourself that the actions you're taking are appropriate is enough to release feelings of guilt. However, what if you feel that the actions you're taking are not appropriate? Should you feel guilty then? The answer is no. Guilt won't help the situation, but creating an action plan will. Ask yourself, "What actions can I take to make positive changes?" Add them to your action plan and then follow through.

Be Curious Instead of Self-Critical

When we have unmet needs, we can become very sensitive to triggers. When you have a strong negative reaction to something, the goal is to become curious instead of self-critical. What could be the reason behind your reaction? Maybe you have some unrealistic expectations of motherhood. Perhaps, like many moms, you haven't been getting enough rest. Maybe you need to ask for support or implement some of the self-care strategies we covered in Chapter 9. Identify your needs and look for healthy ways to fulfill them. Instead of being critical ("I yelled at my child; I'm such a bad mom"), try being curious. Ask yourself, "What do I need right now?"

Make Amends

Everyone makes mistakes. So does that mean you should feel guilty? Absolutely not. Self-reproach isn't productive, but making amends is. It takes courage to admit you did something wrong. But you are one brave Mama Bear. You have the strength to apologize, take responsibility for your actions, and decide to modify future behavior.

Ask yourself, "Do I need to make amends?" I needed to make amends for yelling at my daughter Brianna the way I did. I apologized to her and told her it was wrong for me to behave that way. We hugged, and I told her what I would do differently next time—I would come upstairs to investigate what was happening. Sometimes the best we can do is acknowledge we've made a mistake, learn from it, and move on.

Learn from Mistakes

To learn from mistakes, ask yourself, "What did I learn from this mistake, and what will I do differently next time?" When you learn from your actions and pre-determine what you'll do differently next time, you turn the "mistake" into something of value. Be confident that the next time you're faced with a similar situation, you now have the experience and tools to turn things around. You can feel good about that preparation, Mama Bear. Learn from your mistakes to release guilt.

The bottom line is this: What you think determines what you feel. For that reason, when you're feeling guilty, check in with your thoughts. Ask yourself, "Is the word 'should' at the root of my guilty feelings? Is it true? Is it fact? It is helpful? Am I doing the best I can? Is what I'm doing appropriate in this situation? What do I need right now? Do I need to make amends? What did I learn from this mistake, and what will I do differently next time?"

Hats off to you. Becoming a mom changes everything. Whether you gave birth to your child, adopted your child, or stepped into the role as stepmom—you're caring for the future humans of our planet. Your role as mom is an ultra-important one. It's tough enough without adding guilt to the mix, so give yourself the right to be human.

You're doing great. You've got this!

CHAPTER 14

Let Go of Judgment

The "Mom-Shaming" Edition

Six days after my first daughter, Lindsay, was born, I came down with a fever of 104. I was freezing, and no matter how many socks and blankets I piled on, I couldn't get warm. My husband called the hospital, and they told him to bring me in right away. The diagnosis was mastitis. My right breast was inflamed, painful, and hot. I was admitted into the hospital, and the doctors started me on intravenous antibiotics.

"What about my baby?" I asked. "I'm breastfeeding."

"She can stay in the hospital with you," I was told.

Over the next couple of days, doctors and nurses came in and out of my room to check on me. While they did that, they'd *also* give me their advice on feeding my baby.

"You can't breastfeed while you're on these antibiotics," one doctor said. "It's not good for the baby."

Oh no! I don't want to hurt my baby, I thought. *I'd better stop!*

After I asked for formula, another doctor said, "You can't stop breastfeeding now. The medication won't hurt the baby."

Oh no! I don't want to switch to formula if that's not what's best for my baby.

"I brought you some formula," said another. "You really shouldn't be breastfeeding now."

What on earth am I supposed to do?

The medical opinions on what was best for my infant went back and forth like a ping-pong ball in an Olympic-level match, and not only did I have to make a decision based on this confusing information, I had to do so while I was in pain, exhausted, and caring for my newborn. That's not the easiest foundation from which to make a good decision. But there are times in every mom's life when she has to decide what is right for her child even when the options aren't clear and the timing isn't optimal.

Here's how I decided. Some doctors said the antibiotics could hurt my baby. While some said it wouldn't, was I willing to take that chance on my beautiful newborn? I was fed formula as a baby, and I'm healthy. Millions of babies around the world are fed formula, and they do okay. I made up my mind and switched to formula.

Some moms reading this now will be thinking, "Oh yes! I agree with you. I would have switched too." Others will be thinking, "Oh no! Not me. I would have continued breastfeeding." And that's okay! Every mom is entitled to her own opinion. But be aware, when you feel the need to express your unsolicited opinions to other mothers, you might be entering the mom-shaming zone.

The Mom-Shaming Zone

Mom-shaming is everywhere: it runs wild on social media, slithers around neighborhood parks, and even rears its ugly head in supermarkets, shopping malls, and checkout lines. But what is it exactly? Mom-shaming is criticizing (or even degrading) other moms for making parenting choices different than our own.

Why do moms shame other moms? Some do it unintentionally. They truly believe their way of doing things is the right way. They're convinced they must share their opinions with you because it will help you. Others use it as a form of control—like bullies from our childhoods. Bullies use rude comments and biting sarcasm to gain and keep some sort of perceived status. And then there are those who shame other moms in order to make themselves feel better about their own parenting choices.

There are no winners in the mom-shaming arena. It hurts both the mom being judged and the mom doing the judging. Think of it this way: negative judgments require us to focus on flaws and weaknesses rather than strengths. Dwelling on negatives erodes your peace of mind and builds inner turmoil. When you find yourself judging someone to make yourself feel better about your own choices, try to remember that what someone else has or hasn't done does not undo what you have or haven't done.

Finally, the more you judge others, the more critical you become of yourself. Judging others becomes a comparison trap. When you compare someone else's choices, actions, or beliefs to your own, you run the risk of coming up short. Ironically, people are often most critical of others in the areas in which they themselves are the weakest. Judging someone to feel better about your own perceived shortcomings can end up shining a spotlight on the things you dislike most about yourself.

Ugh! Mom-shaming. It has to stop. It's time to let go of judgment. Before you speak up and share your opinions to—or about—another mom and her parenting choices, follow these dos and don'ts. That way you can ensure you do become part of the solution and don't become part of the problem.

Be the Solution: The Do's and Don'ts

Don't Comment on Mom's Body Shape or Weight

Here's what full-on mom-shaming can sound like:

"She *still* hasn't lost her baby weight? Is she just sitting around all day?"

Or . . .

"She lost the baby weight *already*? Does she ever look after her child, or is she always at the gym?"

Yikes! Do you notice there's no way to succeed in the eyes of this mom-shamer?

For us kinder, gentler, more loving friends who wouldn't dream of intentionally shaming another woman that way, it's still wise to avoid commenting on a mom's body shape or weight. Because our society is so focused on appearance, that can be challenging. Telling a new mom "You look great now that you've lost all the baby weight!" can seem like a harmless compliment. However, weight and appearance can be incredibly triggering for many women. If you want to compliment a mom, there are better ways.

Do Encourage Mom with Non-Appearance-Based Compliments

We could all use some encouragement. Encourage other moms—and yourself—with genuine non-appearance-based compliments. Here are some examples:

"You're a really great mom."

"Your kids are fortunate to have you as their mom."

"You're such a loving and strong mom!"

Come up with some examples of your own and begin encouraging moms in the areas that truly matter.

Instead of:	Try:
You look like you've lost weight.	I see how much you love your child.
Wow! You washed your hair. You look so nice.	You're a really great mom!

Don't Judge Mom for Taking Time for Herself

"Why does she send her child to daycare once a week? She doesn't even work!"

Hey, that's shady, lady! Taking care of children is one of the hardest jobs on the planet. A little self-care goes a long way. If Mama Bear has this option and is taking advantage of it, bravo!

Do Support Mom's Choice of Self-Care

Making time for self-care helps protect a mom's emotional, mental, and physical health. A healthy mom is better equipped to deal with the challenges and demands of raising kids. Support a mom's choice of self-care. Better yet, if you see a mom struggling to find time for self-care, offer to help with her kids. Whether she chooses to rest by taking a nap or to recharge by having coffee with good friends, support her choice to take care of her well-being no matter what self-care methods you prefer.

Don't Question Mom's Child's Development

"He *still* isn't potty trained?"

"She *still* uses a soother?"

Even though you may have the best of intentions, you're not helping by questioning a child's milestones. Moms are very aware of when specific milestones are typically reached. She's likely Googled it or read about it and is more worried about it than you know. By questioning her child's development, you're just adding to her stress.

Do Acknowledge Every Child Develops at a Slightly Different Rate

Instead, acknowledge that every child develops at a slightly differ-ent rate—to yourself if you haven't specifically been asked for your opinion. If her child is happy, healthy, and well-loved, trust that Mama Bear is on top of her child's growth and development and that if she has concerns, she will talk to an expert.

Listen, a toddler can log into a password-protected iPad and find their favorite cartoon. I'm pretty sure preschoolers could perform a bank heist if there was a cookie stash in the vault. Her child will figure out a toilet when he is good and ready!

Don't Question Mom's Parenting Choices

Moms make an overwhelming number of parenting decisions daily. It's tough enough without others poking their noses in with their own opinions. Here's an example of what not to say: "Is frozen pizza all that you're feeding your family for dinner tonight? Do you add a salad or something? I have a great recipe for healthy pizza." The message you're conveying is that you have a better way and that what she is doing isn't enough.

Besides, do you really think your "soy-based alternative" will get past her child, the one who gave the mall Santa side-eye for wearing burgundy instead of true red? She knows she has a child with the eyes of a falcon and an appetite for frozen pizza, and she's doing what she needs to in order to keep that child fed.

Do Recognize Mom Is Doing Her Best

Even if what you think you're saying will help, quite often what you're actually doing is making Mama Bear feel bad about her choices. So what if she made a frozen pizza for her child's dinner while you made a gluten-free, vegan, organic one? She knows her kids! They won't eat the cheeseless flatbread or the broccoli stems hidden in the "pizza sauce" no matter what the good people on the fancy websites promise. You know what they *will* eat? Frozen pizza.

Listen, I'm all for a good cauliflower crust, but if you can see Mama Bear has a happy, healthy, well-loved child, it's best to keep your recommendations to yourself.

The good news is that the more you release harsh judgments instead of sharing them, the more peace of mind and contentment you'll experience on a regular basis. The less you condemn others, the less you will condemn yourself. You'll be able to live your own life and parent your own children with greater self-love, self-acceptance, and inner calm.

Strategies for Dealing with Being Mom-Shamed

Mama Bear, making parenting decisions can be tiring. It can end up being even more exhausting when you're faced with the possibly of displeasing others, being criticized, or being shamed for your choices. For that reason, here are some strategies to help you deal with the unwanted advice, unsolicited criticism, and unhelpful opinions of others so that you can make the parenting decisions you feel are best for you and your family with more confidence, less worry, and greater inner peace.

First, consider the source. Who is criticizing you? Is it someone you trust? Is it someone who wants the best for you? What gives this person credibility? Constructive criticism can help you grow, but you don't have to accept criticism from just anyone. When something someone has said upsets you, make sure to consider the source. You will feel your best if you spend your time with people who inspire you, believe in you, and want to support you just the way you are.

> You have immense value and incredible worth—and that is true regardless of what anyone else thinks.

Care about what you think of yourself. You can let go of trying to please everyone else. It's not possible anyway. As my mom often said to me, "The people who love you are going to like you no matter what you do. But there will always be some people who won't like you no matter what you do. You can't please everybody." You have immense value and incredible worth—and that is true regardless of what anyone else thinks. When faced with the choice of caring about what others think of you or caring about what you think of yourself, I strongly recommend you choose you. You're marvelous!

Look at the bigger picture. When you're faced with criticism, instead of focusing on negative comments, step back and take a look at the bigger picture. Ask yourself, "In my opinion, what do I think I have done well? What am I doing right?" Let the answers to these questions help you acknowledge and appreciate all of the ways and all of the areas in which you're succeeding. Doing so will go a long way toward helping you restore your peace of mind. Yes, sometimes criticism can carry hidden valuable feedback. However, one negative comment, no matter how correct or incorrect it may be, does not reflect the entire story.

Finally, stand your ground. You can stand firm in your choices. You don't have to argue your point of view or defend your decisions. Who has time for that anyway? Breathe easy knowing that you're doing your best and your best is enough.

The next time criticism is eroding your inner peace, making you doubt yourself, or making you feel bad about your parenting choices, remember to consider the source, care more about what you think of yourself, look at the bigger picture, and stand your ground.

CHAPTER 15

Let Go of Perfectionism

The "Good Moms Make Mistakes" Edition

"Come into the living room," said my husband. My two daughters, then seven and five, stood beside him, giggling. "I got you something, and you're going to want to sit down for this."

I sat down, and from behind his back he pulled out a red-and-white plastic bag from a bookstore.

I love books, I thought, *but why on earth would I need to sit down for something that comes from a bookstore?*

I took the bag and looked inside to see a book on how to train your German shepherd puppy.

He bought me a German shepherd? I was conflicted.

I'd recently asked a neighbor if I could take her German shepherd out for walks, but I only wanted to walk her dog so I would feel safe on long walks by myself, then come back to my perfectly clean, dog-hair-free house when I was finished. My husband, however, thought my request meant I wanted a German shepherd of my own.

Gung ho on his assumption, my husband had researched breeders and made a hefty down payment on a puppy. All I had to do was choose the one I wanted from the litter.

As I held the book and looked at the huge smiles on my husband's and daughters' faces, I thought, *I don't want a dog. There will be too much dog hair. I love my clean house . . . but look at their smiles. It's a very thoughtful gift. And I do love dogs. It could be good for our family to have a pet. Okay, I'm getting a dog!*

When we visited the breeder's place, I immediately noticed the cutest little puppy jumping at the baby gate containing the litter. He whined, wagged, and wiggled as he made his best attempts to get at us through the gate. We named him Cody and took him home.

It didn't take long for me to realize the thoughts I'd had while holding that book were all correct: *It really is good for our family to have a pet. The girls adore this puppy. And there's way too much dog hair!*

Oh, the dog hair! If you are unfamiliar with the German shepherd breed, they are gorgeous seventy-five-pound dogs with black-and-brown coats that shed one hundred fifty pounds of fur. Daily. Not a rough estimate. Okay, I'm exaggerating here. But my perfectly clean home was no longer perfectly clean—and it was completely stressing me out. But what could I do? We vacuumed the house regularly and had Cody groomed frequently. But as long as we had a dog in the house, the dog hair wasn't going anywhere. The dog wasn't going anywhere either. We loved Cody, and I certainly wasn't going to let him go. The only thing I could let go of was my perfectionism.

Perfectionism can be intensified by motherhood. Things change in the blink of an eye the day you become a mom. Maybe, like me, you were used to having your home in order. But now there is a baby, and you don't have the time or energy to get to the dishes in the sink, or the bottles on the counter, or the laundry piling up, and it's weighing on you because you think you should be able to do more, to do better, to be better.

Perhaps your kids are in school, and now there are constantly toys, artwork, paperwork, clothes, shoes, and backpacks to pick up. There are lunches to make, homework to help finish, arguments to referee, problems to help solve, dance recitals and team practices to shuttle the kids to and from, boo-boos to kiss, and broken hearts to help mend—and maybe (and that's a big maybe) now that the kids are older, you have more time to attend to all of these things, but you're still feeling burnt out. Why? It's because managing your own life, in addition to everything that comes along with parenting, is a ton of work. Trying to manage all of these things perfectly is downright exhausting.

How about you? Are you a perfectionist? Are you a "recovering" perfectionist? Are you not answering because you're afraid of responding incorrectly? Regardless of your answer, one thing is certain: perfectionism breeds worry and erodes inner peace.

But isn't it good to have high standards? Sure it is. High standards can serve you well. Doing your best has its rewards. However, when you feel like no matter how hard you try, it's never good enough—or that you are never good enough—those standards are working against you. Perfectionism works against you in several ways:

First, it can lead to procrastination. For example, maybe you put off doing something because you don't think you'll be able to do it perfectly. You might think, *If I can't do it perfectly, I won't do it all.*

Second, perfectionism can stop you from asking for help. For example, you might hold the popular (and limiting) belief, "If I want something done right, I'd better do it myself," even when sometimes, if you want a thing done at all, you have to ask someone else to help you complete it! Or you might think, *If I ask for help, others will think less of me because I should be able to do all of this all by myself.*

Third, perfectionism can cause you to become self-critical. You think, *What's wrong with me? I burned the toast again, I got the kids to school late, and I forgot to put last night's clean laundry into the dryer. Why do I always make mistakes? If I was a good mom, the meals would be perfect, our family would never be late, and the kids would always be happy.*

And finally, perfectionism can leave you feeling burnt out as you constantly strive to be "perfect" in an effort to please everyone else.

Where does perfectionism come from? Sometimes perfectionism is rooted in childhood experiences in which you needed to obsessively plan for various scenarios in order to feel safe. I certainly needed a defense mechanism as a child, so I developed perfectionistic traits that I kept as an adult. My father was an alcoholic, which resulted in some chaos in my home life. At school, I was teased and bullied. The place I felt safest was in my bedroom. I gained a sense of control despite the chaos by organizing every toy in my room, making my bed, dusting my shelves, and even vacuuming my floor well before I was ten years old. Then I brought that need for a perfectly organized and clean environment into adulthood (hence my dilemma with the dog hair).

Other times, perfectionism is driven by the belief that acceptance from others is conditional. You conclude that in order to be accepted, you must be perfect. During my childhood, in addition to seeking control through order, I also developed a limiting belief that unless I was perfect, I was unlovable. So I strived for perfection in every area of my life in order to gain love and approval from my parents, teachers, and friends. I strived for perfection in my grades. I strived for perfection in my appearance, which led to eating disorders and low self-esteem. But I didn't expect perfection from anyone else. I only demanded it from myself.

Many of us have had moments in our lives that have shaped our beliefs about who we are. Our memories of these moments can be very vivid. Your moments may have caused you to believe that you're not good enough, you don't belong, you're on your own, or that there's something wrong with you. I want to tell you right here and right now: You are enough! You do belong! You're not alone! There isn't anything wrong with you! Mama Bear, I know you're not perfect. I'm not either.

> Nobody is perfect. The good news is that while there is no way to be a perfect mom, there are hundreds of ways to be a good one.

Nobody is perfect. The good news is that while there is no way to be a perfect mom, there are hundreds of ways to be a good one. One way to be a good mom is to do your best to let go of perfectionism. Here are some strategies to help you begin the process of breaking free from the shackles of perfectionism.

Adjust Your Self-Talk

Perfectionists understand that attaining perfection isn't possible, but they try anyway. When they fall short, their inner critic is ever on the alert, ready to point out every perceived mistake and flaw. In the mind of a perfectionist, "I made a mistake" turns into "I failed," which turns into "I am a failure." You learned about the difference between fact and opinion in Chapter 2. Is it a fact or an opinion that making a mistake makes you a failure? It's an opinion—and a very limiting one at that.

Mama Bear, you are not your mistakes. You are not a failure. You are enough! It's time to silence that inner voice that tells you that anything less than 100% isn't good enough. That voice isn't telling you the truth! Here are some adjustments you can make to your self-talk to silence that voice.

Instead of:	Try:
I'm such a bad mom.	I am a good mom. I am the mom my kids need.
I messed up.	I didn't like that choice. I'll do it differently next time.
I always make mistakes.	I made a mistake. I'll learn from it and do better next time.
I yelled at my child. I'm terrible.	I wonder why I reacted that way. What do I need right now?
I'm not a good enough mom.	I am a present and loving mom. I am enough.
I'm a failure.	I love who I am and who I'm becoming.
What's wrong with me?	What's *right* with me?
I didn't do everything right.	I may not have done everything right, but I didn't do everything wrong either.

Aim for Connection Instead of Perfection

Human beings need connection. In her book titled *Cleaning Up Your Mental Mess: 5 Simple, Scientifically Proven Steps to Reduce Anxiety, Stress, and Toxic Thinking*, Dr. Caroline Leaf writes, "When we engage with others, our cortisol levels go down while the neurotransmitters serotonin and dopamine balance in our brains. We have higher levels of all the brain waves that promote healing and lower levels of anxiety-linked high beta. We feel good subjectively, and this translates into changes in our cells. Mind becomes matter as our brains are flooded with pleasure-inducing endorphins, intimacy-producing oxytocin, and the bliss molecule anandamide."[20] Now you know why it feels so uplifting to spend time with a good friend! Connection heals.

Has perfectionism stopped you from connecting with others? For instance, have you ever avoided getting on a Zoom call with a friend because you think you don't look good enough (aka "perfect") or your home in the background isn't tidy enough (aka "perfect")? It makes you wonder why you upgraded your phone when your four-megapixel phone from high school would blur out that laundry pile and your freshly cut anxiety bangs. To toss out perfection, think of your home as a modern art exhibition: Your artistically arranged laundry basket on the couch elegantly offsets your child practicing recorder in the background, which tells the story of the fragility of one woman's last nerve. The truth is that unless your home has recently been overrun by brain-eating zombies, we've seen it all before.

Your children and your true friends are not concerned with the state of your house, the shape of your body, the brand of clothes you wear, the kind of car you drive, or whether you or your family are photo ready. What they care about is *you*. You are safe to be yourself. Go ahead and connect with others just as you are right now.

In fact, the most effective way to connect with others is by sharing your vulnerabilities. Perfectionism will have you working overtime to maintain an appearance of "having it all together." Well, guess what? You actually connect best with others when you admit you don't.

In his book *Get Off Your "But": How to End Self-Sabotage and Stand Up for Yourself*, Sean Stephenson wrote, "Trying to appear perfect and superior kills connection. Think about it. When was the last time you heard someone talk on and on about his accomplishments and strengths and you ended up feeling closer to him? Never. We bond through our imperfections and shortcomings. Authenticity and vulnerability are the glue of connection."[21]

This means you don't have to wait until you look better, or the house is tidier. You can start connecting right now! If it feels scary, push through the fear. Don't worry about trying to pretend you "have it all together." Nobody does. Listen, I'm the Worry

Management Expert, and sometimes I bite my fingernails! See? I have flaws too. I'm perfectly imperfect.

Be your perfectly imperfect self and pick a date to go for a walk with that friend you've been wanting to see for ages. Text your bestie to set up a video chat or a coffee date.

Connection with others builds joy in our lives. Perfection, on the other hand, robs us of our inner peace. Connection heals and perfection steals. Throw on some comfortable clothes and get connecting with people you love.

Think Progress, Not Perfection

During that time of chaos in my childhood, I won the most amazing T-shirt at summer camp. On the front, it said, "Be patient. God hasn't finished with me yet."

That shirt gave me such peace. Knowing I was a "work in progress" helped me to not believe the things those bullies were saying to and about me. It didn't matter what they said, because God wasn't finished with me yet. I'm still a work in progress, and so are you!

When perfectionism tries to tear you down, think progress, not perfection. You didn't accomplish every single thing you had planned to do today? That's okay! Think progress, not perfection. Where did you make progress? What did you complete? You might find it helpful to write the answers to those questions in a journal. Having a record of your progression can help you to see how far you've really come and how much progress you're actually making. Some days, the only answer you write down might be "I made it through a tough day today." Hey, Mama Bear, sometimes making it through a tough day is progress enough. Be patient with yourself. You are a work in progress, and you—and the progress you've made—are enough!

Accept "What Is"

Life is never going to be perfect. Many times we wish our lives away by wanting things to be different than they are right now. By all means, take action to control the things you can and then let go of the things you can't by accepting "what is."

Accepting "what is" doesn't mean you have to like "what is." For instance, I was able to get to a place where I was able to accept the dog hair. I didn't like the dog hair, but I was able to accept it because it and my dog—something I loved very much—were a package deal.

To accept "what is," I adjusted my focus. I focused on the joy the dog brought to our family, and I focused my attention on the things I *could* keep clean in the house. You see, one day, it dawned on me: *I can just focus on the house from the baseboards up. Yes, we'll vacuum and get Cody groomed consistently. But from now on, I'm looking up.*

Isn't it time you looked up too? Look up from your perceived flaws and shortcomings. Start to see yourself as the awesome mother you are—the one who loves her children to the moon and back. Look up and accept "what is."

Get Comfortable Making Mistakes

Let's face it: mistakes are inevitable. But beating yourself up over them is optional. Getting comfortable making mistakes will help you to recover more quickly from them when they happen. On top of that, the more comfortable you are with making mistakes, the more comfortable your child will become with making mistakes. It makes life more enjoyable and freeing for both of you. How do you get comfortable making mistakes? Try the following suggestions on for size.

Make more mistakes. What? Make more mistakes? That's right! The more mistakes you make, the less afraid you'll become of making them. I'm not suggesting you make mistakes on purpose or that you take foolish risks. I'm suggesting you don't allow the *possibility* of making a mistake stop you from taking action.

Think of it this way: Making a mistake is a good sign that you are doing something right; it proves you're at least doing something! To have the most opportunity to grow and succeed, you don't need to do everything perfectly. To grow and succeed, you need to make mistakes fast and learn from them even faster. That brings us to the second suggestion.

Learn from your mistakes. One of my favorite scenes in the Walt Disney animated film *Meet the Robinsons* is the one where Lewis (a young boy) tries a new invention out in front of his family, and it doesn't work. He is beating himself up over it when his family interrupts him with cheers: "You failed!" they exclaim. "And it was awesome! Exceptional! Outstanding! From failing you learn. From success, not so much."

Think about it: penicillin, cornflakes, dating that guy because he drove a motorcycle—all are technically mistakes, but they have made us stronger—and gave us at least one cool story to tell at parties.

The next time you make a mistake, rather than beating yourself up over it, ask yourself, "What did I learn from this experience, and what will I do differently next time?" When you learn from your mistakes, you grow. You become stronger and wiser!

Make decisions and take actions in alignment with your values. Doing so can help you to feel more at peace with the outcomes of your actions. You'll know you did the best you could and that the choice you made came from the desire to do what was right. That's something you can feel good about—even if you didn't get the outcome you had hoped for.

Go after what you want *without* striving for perfection. Take action, and if you get the outcome you were hoping for, that's great! If not, pat yourself on the back for doing your best, then learn what you can and adjust your actions until you get the result you want. Despite my many, many, many mistakes, this very approach keeps me growing forward. It will help you to grow forward too!

Enjoy a Perfectly Imperfect Life

Letting go of perfectionism is a process, and that process won't be perfect (pun intended). Be patient with yourself as you adjust your self-talk, aim for connection and progress, accept "what is," and get comfortable making mistakes. Patience in the process will help you to bring increased calm into your life even in the middle of chaos.

As for me and my dog, that puppy turned out to be an even better gift than I'd originally anticipated. He loved us, protected us, and taught me how to begin letting go of my own perfectionism. In fact, I became so comfortable with my perfectly imperfect dog-hair situation that when Cody was only eighteen months old, I made the decision to rescue a five-year-old female German shepherd from the dog pound. I ended up with two dogs, twice the fur, and much more than twice the love.

To ease some of the stress from the work and messiness that comes along with motherhood, do what you can to set more realistic standards for yourself and your family. Letting go of perfectionism leaves so much more space in your life for fun, happiness, and oodles of love!

CHAPTER 16

Let Go of Fear

The "Faith over Fear" Edition

It was the first snowfall of the winter, and I had just returned from a holiday in Disney World with my husband and two young daughters. That day is a day I'll never forget!

My family was home and settling into post-vacation mode. The bags were unpacked and laundry was being done, so I went to the hairdresser. I exited the salon to discover more than five centimeters of fresh snow blanketing my two-month-old car and the road. I cleared off the car and began to make my way home. I was driving slowly, and other vehicles were lining up behind me because of my speed. I could imagine their frustration: "C'mon, lady! It's just a little snow!" But I continued driving at that pace because it gave me a feeling of safety.

I was approaching an intersection at which I had the right-of-way, with stop signs on the intersecting road. But what the driver approaching the stop sign to the left didn't know was that the road under the snow was covered in a sheet of ice. It was an accident waiting to happen. The driver applied the brakes, and their vehicle began to slide at full speed through the intersection. They were out of control!

My brakes were no match for the ice either. As our vehicles slid toward each other, time slowed down—it was like being in slow motion. Have you seen the movie *The Matrix*? Time slows down to a point where the characters can see speeding bullets moving slow enough that they can dodge them. If you were witnessing this accident, it would have seemed to happen in a snap. In an instant. But for me, time had really slowed down.

As the other car slid toward me, I thought, *This isn't going to be good. Am I going to die now?*

Time slowed down so much, I contemplated whether I could undo my seat belt and climb into the back seat for protection.

I thought, *I don't want to die.*

Then I heard a voice. The voice seemed like my own voice, but it was coming from the back of my mind. It asked one question: *Why?*

Because I want to be there for my kids.

Crunch. The other vehicle smashed into mine.

I want to write more books.

Crunch. I could see the metal of my car crushing inward toward my body.

I want to speak to more audiences and help more people.

Crunch.

I've never been to England.

BAM! The airbags deployed. My car had been pushed off the road and into a field. The engine was still going. There was smoke. I thought the car might explode, and I wanted to get out, but I thought my legs were broken—they hurt, and the front of the car was pushed in on me.

Then I looked out the driver's-side window and saw a blond-haired guy standing right beside me. It struck me that he wasn't wearing winter attire and it was really cold outside. He looked like a healthy, surfer-type guy, dressed for a day at the beach. He didn't speak to me, but the way he looked into my eyes felt like *love* and *concern*. It's hard to explain, but I felt then that he cared very much about me and was asking me—with just his expression—"Are you okay?"

I said, "Can you help me get out of the car?" I turned away from his face and looked down at my legs.

When I looked back up, he was gone. My heart raced with fear that my car would explode. I wanted to get out.

I heard a woman yelling, "Get away from her car. She doesn't want to talk to you!"

She was talking to the driver of the car that hit me, who was walking toward my car, probably to see if I was okay. I thought, *It's okay. I'm not mad. It was an accident. I just want out of this car, now.*

The woman who yelled had witnessed the entire accident. She ran over to my window before the other driver got there. "Are you alright?"

"I need to get out of the car," I replied.

She helped me out and walked me to her vehicle. I sat beside her in the passenger seat as she called 911 and then began asking me questions: "What's your name? Do you have any kids? How old are they? What are their names?"

I knew she was trying to keep me awake and alert by asking me these questions. I answered to be polite, but I was suddenly so tired. All I really wanted to do was to close my eyes and sleep.

While she was asking me these questions, I saw the surfer dude again, standing outside of her car on my side. He was looking at me with that same love and concern I had sensed from him moments earlier.

I thought, *This guy is so nice. He must be her boyfriend, and he's letting me sit here in his seat. It's freezing outside. He doesn't even have a coat on. He must be so cold.*

The woman continued to ask me questions until the ambulance arrived and took me to the hospital. Luckily for me, though my car was totaled, I had escaped with no major injuries. My legs were bruised (but that was from the plastic that had flown off when the airbags deployed), my nose was swollen from the airbag popping me in the face, and my shoulder hurt from where the seat belt had grabbed my body to keep me safely in place—but that was all. It was a miracle! The doctor gave me a clean bill of health and sent me home.

On the way back home and later that night, I continued to wonder about that surfer dude, who didn't say a word but conveyed so much love directly into my spirit.

The next day, the principal of my daughters' school phoned me. "Denise, are you okay?" he asked. "I heard you were in a car accident."

"How did you know? I haven't told anyone yet."

"My daughter was the one who helped you at the accident," he said. "She was just coming home from a first-aid course at the college. When she got home last night, she told us all about the accident and described how she had asked this woman question after question. When I heard the answers, I said to her, 'I think you're talking about Lindsay and Brianna's mom, Denise Marek!'"

I said, "I want to thank your daughter *and* her boyfriend. What's her boyfriend's name?"

But he said, "Denise, she was alone."

It turns out there was no blond-haired surfer dude at the accident scene. The occupants of the other vehicle were bundled up in winter clothing. The girl who helped me was female, and no one else stopped. I was the only one who saw him.

However, I know now that his daughter and I were both far from alone on that day.

Having read this story, who—or what—do you think that blond man with love and compassion in his eyes was? I know what I believe I saw.

For me, I believe it was an angel. Psalms 91:11 says, "For He will command His angels concerning you to guard you in all your ways." This means God promises that His angels will watch over individuals and the situations they find themselves in. His angels have a purpose: to guard His children.

I know what I saw, and I know what I felt that day . . . and it was a miracle. A real-life, God-given miracle—to me.

Have Faith

This accident happened years ago. I'm sharing this story with you now because I understand that motherhood can feel lonely at times. It can be scary. It can be unpredictable. It can be exhausting. When loneliness weighs on you, fear not, for God will never leave you. When you feel like you're losing the battle, fear not, for He is fighting for you. When guilt consumes you, fear not, for God has redeemed you. When you feel you're too exhausted to go on, fear not, for He will strengthen you.

I've heard it said that "fear is faith in reverse." It makes sense then that a remedy for fear is faith. After you have taken all the actions you can to control the controllable—when all that's left for you to do is let go—have faith.

Have faith that God has good plans for your life, plans to give you hope and a good future. Have faith in a favorable outcome for any worrisome situation. Miracles happen every day: Someone with cancer hears from the doctor that the cancer is in remission. A woman who has had difficulty conceiving finds out she's pregnant or adopts her first child. A mom whose child has been battling addiction celebrates that child's first year of sobriety.

When you find yourself smack-dab in the middle of a worrisome situation, calm your mind by having faith that a favorable outcome can happen for you too.

When dealing with a difficult situation, challenge your assumptions, take action to control what you can control, and let go of the uncontrollable by turning your problem over to God.

I believe that God sent me an angel that day. While I was trapped in that twisted wreck of a car, He wanted me to know that I wasn't alone—He was by my side, and He is by your side now. Think of that the next time fear knocks at your door. Calm your mind today by believing the best for tomorrow.

Take a Break—Play the *I Spy* Game!

Have you ever played the "I Spy" game? Here's a version you can use now to reinforce the message of faith over fear. Read the following prompts and either write down your answers or say them aloud. If you're pressed for time, choose only one prompt to answer.

I spy with my little eye something that proves I'm not alone.

Look around you. Can you see something in your environment that proves you're not alone? Do you see your child? Do you see the dishes on the counter your child used for breakfast before going to school? Do you see messages from friends or family on your cell phone? As I said earlier, motherhood can feel lonely at times. Have faith, Mama Bear, that you're not alone. And although we're playing the "I Spy" game, you don't even have to see physical evidence of this for it to be true.

I spy with my little eye something that's an answer to prayer.

Reflect on a time you received an answer to a specific prayer. What was the answer? Did it come in the form of something you read, saw, heard, or experienced? Can you see or remember it now? Maybe you prayed for peace from your worries, and now you're holding this book—filled with strategies to help you—in your hands at this very moment. That's an answer to a prayer. When you're dealing with a worrisome situation, calm your mind by remembering that you've had answers to your prayers in the past and by having faith that your prayers will be answered in the future too.

I spy with my little eye something that shows my strength.

Being a strong mom isn't about how much weight you can lift at the gym. It's about the way you love and care for your littles. Look around. What do you see as evidence of your love? Do you see photos of your smiling kids at the dance recitals and sporting events that you drive them to and from regardless of how tired you may feel? In your mind's eye, can you see the boundaries, curfews, and rules you've set to protect your children? Can you see the values you've instilled in them and the unconditional love you have for them? That's true strength, and you're one strong Mama Bear! When you need strength in the future, have faith that you'll get what you need to help you through.

Enjoy Your Clean Closet

Congratulations! Now you are officially equipped with tools to help you to let go of upset feelings, hurts and offenses, mom-guilt, judgment, perfectionism, and fear. You're free to put down the burdens of the past, the fear of the future, and the uncontrollable things you're dealing with in the present.

It's important to recognize that letting go is like cleaning your closet. It feels impossible until it's done. Then you can't believe how good it feels . . . until a few months later when you need to do it again. What I mean by that is this: you may find yourself taking those burdens that you just put down and picking them back up again.

If that happens, it's okay! Go back and reread the chapters in this part (or check out the Transformation Tracking Sheets in Part 5) and implement the strategies again to help you to let go and move forward. In fact, let's keep moving forward now—right into Part 4. You're about to learn how to master your mind—transform negative thinking and worry starts shrinking.

PART 4

Master Your
Mind

Transform negative thinking and worry starts shrinking.

C ould you be a born worrier? The answer is yes! In November 1996, the discovery of a "worry gene" made front-page news in the *New York Times*.[22] The article reported on a study, published by the journal *Science*, that had identified a certain gene associated with worry.

This "worry gene" has a long version and a short version. If you get the short end of the stick—that is, the short version of this gene—you could be more prone to worry, anxiety, and negative thinking. But take it from me: even if you're more genetically prone, there's still hope! Negative and unhealthy patterns of thought can be broken, no matter how deeply entrenched. You can build new, healthy thought patterns that lead to less worry and greater inner peace. You can literally renew your mind! This is what you'll accomplish in the final step of the CALM process: Master Your Mind.

Mastering your mind is about transforming negative thinking. It's about learning to talk to yourself constructively instead of destructively. Learning to do this is crucial because your inner dialogue is what largely dictates whether you feel worried or calm. Think of it this way: if your thoughts are more negative and fear-based, you'll likely think your way into feeling worried. If your thoughts are more positive and faith-based, you'll likely talk yourself into feeling calm.

The strategies in this section will help you change your thoughts on such a level that even your automatic responses to circumstances that have caused you to feel fearful, worried, or distressed in the past will change for the better. For instance, in settings where once you may have criticized yourself with thoughts of "I'm a bad mom," you'll now be equipped to appraise those situations in a more nurturing way by telling yourself, "I'm a good mom who's having a bad day. I am enough. I can handle it! I'm the mom my kids need."

By using the strategies in the following chapters to master your mind, you can break free from strongholds in your thinking that may have been keeping you stuck in a loop of stress and worry.

Are negative thoughts contributing to your stress and worry? Well, today is the day it all turns around for you. Today is the day you begin to take back control of your thinking. Transform negative thinking and worry starts shrinking.

Now, as you begin to master your mind, it's important to remember that to master something is an ongoing process. Just like learning a new language or playing a musical instrument takes practice, so does learning how to master your mind. Initially, it can seem like not a lot is happening, but just because there aren't any signs of progress doesn't mean that big change isn't coming soon.

There's a certain species of Asian bamboo that, after five years of watering and fertilizing the seed, only shows a minuscule amount of growth above the ground. Until those five years are up, it seems like nothing is happening. However, at the start of that sixth year, after five years of watering and fertilizing, the plant suddenly begins to grow so fast that you can actually hear it growing at a rate of two and a half feet per day!

Over a period of about six weeks, this bamboo shoot can reach ninety feet or higher. Vic Johnson writes about this bamboo plant in his book *Day by Day with James Allen*: "The question to ask is did the bamboo grow 90 feet in six weeks or did it grow 90 feet in five years?"[23]

The answer is that it grew ninety feet in five years—five years *plus* six weeks, to be exact. If the seed hadn't been watered and given sunlight and fertile soil during those five years when it looked like nothing was happening, the plant wouldn't have survived. If, during those five years, the seed was dug up to try and figure out what was "wrong" with it, it wouldn't have had a chance. The seed needed all that time and the right conditions to make that rapid six-week growth possible.

To get results, you first have to plant seeds. That's what you'll learn in this part of the book. You'll learn how to plant new, positive "thought-seeds" so that any negative or limiting thinking that has been keeping you stuck, worried, or stressed will begin to be replaced with thoughts that will help you feel more calm, confident, peaceful, loving, and joyous.

Next, just like the bamboo seed must be nurtured with water, fertilizer, and sunshine, you'll learn strategies to nurture your thought-seeds. By nurturing those positive thought-seeds, you're helping to build a magnificent root system of positive thinking that will support your rapid mental and emotional growth when it comes. When the time is right, you'll be growing faster than your sixth grader hitting a growth spurt the day after going shopping for all-new clothes. (By the way, how do children outgrow shoes overnight?)

CHAPTER 17

Choose Your Mindset

How to Override Negative Thoughts to Create Positive Outcomes

When my daughter Brianna was nine years old, I already saw in her the ability to bounce back from challenge and change. Changes in routine, changes in school, and even moving into a new house in a new neighborhood: none of that clouded her optimistic outlook.

Upon spotting this trait in her, I said, "Brianna, you're my little bouncer. You always bounce back."

She replied, "Mom, only *deflated* balls don't bounce."

While she likely wasn't aware of just how wise her words were, what she said was profound. There are times in life when we all can feel a little mentally and emotionally deflated. There are times we can feel a little less confident, a little less optimistic, or a little less positive. These feelings are a normal part of life. It's okay for you to feel the way you do. However, it's important to understand that you don't have to *stay* deflated. With a little training on how to choose your mindset, you'll be able to experience more peace, fun, joy, happiness, and contentment. You'll also be able to bounce back more easily from difficulties, adversity, and setbacks. As motivational guru Zig Ziglar said, "It's not how far you fall, but how high you bounce that counts."[24]

In this chapter, we're diving into the roots of insecurity. You'll begin to learn how to fix the things you say to yourself. You'll gain an understanding of how your thoughts are formed and why you think the way you do. You'll also learn how you can change your focus to feel better and gain a more positive attitude—one that sets you up for success.

To choose your mindset, it's necessary to understand what a mindset is. Simply put, your mindset is your established set of attitudes. Your attitude determines how you interact with the world around you. It determines not only your ability to handle stressful situations but also the amount of joy and pleasure you get out of life. The most successful people in life tend to have great attitudes. Here are some examples of positive attitudes:

Acceptance	Cooperation	Freedom
Affection	Courageousness	Friendliness
Ambition	Decisiveness	Fun
Aspiration	Devotion	Generosity
Candidness	Endurance	Gratefulness
Care	Enthusiasm	Honesty
Cheerfulness	Faithfulness	Humbleness
Confidence	Flexibility	Joyfulness
Consideration	Forgiveness	Kindness

Maturity	Reliability	Strength
Open-mindedness	Responsibility	Sympathy
Optimism	Self-discipline	Thoughtfulness
Perseverance	Selflessness	Tolerance
Positivity	Sensitivity	Trust
Practicality	Sincerity	Willingness

Do you see any of your current attitudes on this list? Can you spot any attitudes you'd like to have?

The great news, Mama Bear, is that attitude is something you can be trained in. In fact, unless trained in it, people can naturally fall into a negative attitude. Fortunately, all adopting a positive attitude starts with is a decision. John C. Maxwell said, "Your attitude is a choice. If you desire to make your day a masterpiece, then you need to have a great attitude. If it's not good now, you need to change it. Make the decision."[25]

Each of us must make the decision to choose the right attitude daily. Oh yes, Mama Bear, you can have an attitude which brings you greater joy, fun, hope, confidence, happiness, and inner peace.

Your decision to choose a positive attitude can ripple out and impact your child's happiness too. In his book *The Power of Attitude*, Mac Anderson writes, "What most people fail to realize is that your attitude not only impacts your happiness and success, it also can impact the happiness and success of all the people around you . . . your family, your friends, and your peers at work. Attitudes truly are contagious, and from time to time we need to ask ourselves . . . 'is mine worth catching?'"[26]

Is your attitude worth catching? If it isn't, it can be! It all starts with a decision to choose a positive attitude daily.

Make the Decision to Choose a Positive Attitude Daily

You have to commit to taking back control of your thinking. You can learn to fix what you say to yourself. However, you have to make the decision to do the work.

A decision is an action. The word "decide" comes from the Latin root *decidere*—meaning "to cut off from." That means when you make a decision, you're cutting off any other alternatives.

When you decide to have an attitude of gratitude, it means you're choosing to cut off—or stop looking for—all the things you think are missing from your life. When you decide to see the best in yourself, it means you're choosing to cut off or stop looking for the things you think you should be doing differently or that you perceive as flaws. Are there any things you need to cut off or stop looking for in your own life?

One of the reasons it's in your best interest to cut off negative thinking is that negative thinking has a nasty way of making you find exactly what you're looking for. Here's a personal example. (It's from my past, so keep in mind that I hadn't yet discovered all of the amazing strategies and techniques you're learning now!)

I was twenty-two years old when my first daughter was born. In the months leading up to her birth, I was really looking forward to having time off from work to enjoy spending it with my new baby in this new stage of my life. I thought, *This will be great! After the baby is born, I'll sleep when she sleeps—or maybe I'll use that time to clean the house, sit in the sunshine, or get back into my fitness routine. I'm just excited to finally have a summer off. It's going to be a wonderful vacation.*

That is *not* what happened. My newborn cried—a lot! I cried—a lot! She rarely slept. I rarely slept. I actually remember thinking, *This is it! The best part of my life is officially over.* Tell me I'm not alone here! Were you totally prepared for the reality of parenting?

A friend of mine from work had given birth two weeks before I did; plus she had a one-year-old to take care of. *I'll call her,* I thought. *She'll be feeling the same way I am, and we can feel miserable together.*

"Hey," I said to my friend when she answered the phone. "What are you doing?"

"Hey, Denise!" she replied, full of rainbows and sunshine. "I just baked chocolate chip cookies, and these cookies are so good. I have to give you this recipe. How about you? What are you up to?"

What? I thought. *How does she have so much energy? She baked cookies? I haven't even showered for the last two days.*

I started mentally comparing how and what I was doing with how and what she was doing. The more I searched for the ways in which she was succeeding and the ways in which I perceived I was failing, the more ways I found, and the worse I felt.

Have you done that too? Have you ever compared yourself with someone—another mom, a friend, a parent on social media—and suddenly you didn't feel so good about yourself anymore? What happened? Well, your thoughts revealed a seed of insecurity.

Recognize Seeds of Insecurity

The root of my negative thoughts was not that my friend was doing well. The real issue was coming from a seed of insecurity that had been planted in my mind years before I became a mom. It was a seed that said, "I'm not good enough."

Seeds of insecurity have been planted in our minds by past experiences and the insecurities others express to us. These seeds can create a defeated mentality that includes thoughts like these: "Nobody likes me." "I'm not good enough." "I don't belong." "Nobody wants me." "Nothing goes my way." "I'll never be happy." "I'll never succeed." Thoughts become feelings, and thoughts like these can cause you to feel deflated.

Human beings take their seeds of insecurity out into the world and go looking for evidence to prove they are true. What do you think happens as a result? Proof is found. Seek and you will find. That being said, the evidence you find—which may seem like it proves that the negative things you believe about yourself are true—doesn't actually make those things true. It might *feel* true—just like when I didn't feel good enough compared to my chocolate-chip-cookie-baking coworker. Yet I was only feeling that way because of the thoughts I was thinking. Feelings are not facts.

You're still a good mom when you feel like you're failing, when you take time out for self-care, when you have a bad day, when you feel angry, or when your child is having a meltdown. You're still a good mom when you need a break, you struggle with mental health, or your child refuses to listen to you. Being a mom is hard. It doesn't mean you're doing anything wrong—even if it *feels* that way.

Understand How Thoughts are Formed

I've said already in this chapter that feelings are an emotional response to the thoughts you're thinking. Think positive thoughts and you feel good. Think negative thoughts and you feel bad. But if we know this, why do we continue to think thoughts that make us feel bad? When we know negative assumptions are driving us to feel worried, why do we jump to the same conclusions over and over? (Listen, contrary to what your fitness tracker is trying to tell you, a raised heartrate from jumping to conclusions is not cardio!)

I was curious too, so for over two decades, I have researched how our thoughts are formed, the thought process, and human ways of thinking. I'm sharing my discoveries with you because when you understand how your thoughts work, you can unravel limiting beliefs that may be keeping you feeling trapped, stuck, or insecure.

Understanding why you think the way you do can help you stop judging yourself harshly for thinking negative thoughts. You'll know what's driving you to think the way you do, which puts you in a better position to change your thinking for the better! If you're interested in a great introduction to how the brain works, I recommend Dr. Caroline Leaf's book *Who Switched Off My Brain? Controlling Toxic Thoughts and Emotions*, which I've quoted from once already. In the meantime, here's what I've learned about how thoughts are formed.

Your thoughts are composed of neurons, chemicals, and electrical impulses. As you grow and develop, these neurons form tree-like branches called dendrites. The things you've heard, the things you seen, and the things you've experienced—your memories—are stored in these dendrites.

Now imagine a forest filled with trees. Picture the branches of the trees growing and intertwining with each other. Imagine that each time you think, those branches grow, get stronger, and intertwine with one another further.

That's what it's like in your mind. As you think, these tree-like branches (dendrites) begin to grow and network with other branches (dendrites) of thoughts and memories. Unlike the branches in the forest, the dendrites in your mind literally connect with each other as they network. Stored memories are physically built into this nerve network of your mind. The more you focus on and contemplate a specific thought, the more branches grow, the more connections deepen, and the more that thought becomes "permanent."

When you've had past experiences that caused you to think "I'm not good enough," "I don't belong," or "I'm not smart enough," one of those tree-like branches grew in your mind. That thought was stored as a permanent memory. The more frequently you reflected on that same thought, the more that branch grew, the stronger it became, the more it networked with other thoughts and memories, and that's how it became permanent.

The permanent nature of our thoughts is why choosing your mindset takes practice. It's also why it's so easy to fall back into negative thought patterns. It's like that bowling ball we talked about in Chapter 2, the one that gets stuck in the gutter. The rut in the gutter is so deep that the ball, once it falls into it, can only follow one path all the way down the lane—unless something or someone stops it. Just like that, our thoughts can get stuck in a neural-pathway rut.

The way your brain makes your thoughts permanent is actually a protection mechanism. Once memories and thoughts are permanent, we use the resultant neural pathways to assess, appraise, and react to situations as quickly and as efficiently as possible. For instance, suppose you touched a hot stove when you were young and got burned. From that pain, you thought, "Ouch! Don't touch a hot stove." That thought is saved as a permanent memory to prevent you from touching a hot stove in the future. It reduces the risk of you getting burned again. That's helpful.

However, some "burns" you get in life are from emotional pain. For example, suppose your partner broke up with you, you got teased at school, or you failed a test. From that emotional pain, you may have concluded that "I'm not good enough," "I don't belong," or "I'm not smart enough." Even though those thoughts were untrue, they still grew. Each time something reinforced the thought (you remembered it, you talked about it, you went through or heard about someone else's breakup, you received some unsolicited criticism about your parenting skills, or you heard that your friend was baking homemade cookies while you were struggling just to get out of your PJs), the more those thought-seeds grew, and the stronger and more permanent they became. That's limiting.

Is it beginning to make sense now why you think the way you do? Thankfully, even though your thoughts have been created in a "permanent" way, permanent does not mean they can *never* be changed.

The Free Dictionary defines "permanent" as "lasting or remaining without essential change" or "not expected to change in status, condition or place."[27] Just because something is "lasting or remaining" or "not expected to change," that doesn't mean it can't be changed. In fact, in this case, it can! Your thoughts are active. They grow *and* they change.

You can grow new, healthy thoughts and allow those more positive branches and connections to deepen and grow. As you work on building new healthy replacement thoughts, the old negative, distressing, and toxic thoughts can die off and go away. You can literally renew your mind!

This doesn't mean insecurities and limiting thoughts won't enter your mind ever again. They will. As you're consciously choosing to think new thoughts, both the old and new thoughts will coexist for a time before the old ones die off. For a while, it's going to be more crowded in there than when your in-laws come to stay—with their cats! This is where your continued effort is required. You need to nurture and reinforce the new positive thoughts even while the old ones are being pruned away. Prune your negative thoughts like a bonsai tree if you must; just get snipping!

So what about these new positive thoughts? How do you plant, nurture, and reinforce these new thought-seeds? Paradoxically, not by covering them with manure. It's by training your thinking, which contains two components: overriding the negative and adjusting your focus.

Train Your Thinking—Override the Negative

Imagine that you and your child have decided to plant a vegetable garden. What kind of vegetables do you want in your garden? Do you want some tomatoes? How about some cucumbers and green beans? Would you like some carrots in there too? Great! That sounds like a lovely garden.

In order to grow those kinds of vegetables, what kinds of seeds do you need? You'll need tomato, cucumber, green bean, and carrot seeds, of course. After planting those seeds and tending to your garden, you'll be eating those delicious vegetables before you know it! However, if you planted dandelion seeds instead, no matter how much you wanted to harvest a good crop of vegetables, all you would get would be weeds. You get what you plant.

The same thing happens when planting thought-seeds. To grow positive feelings, you must plant positive thoughts. To grow a positive attitude, you must plant positive thoughts. A good place to start is by overriding any existing negative thoughts—ways of thinking which are not contributing to the feelings, attitudes, and outcomes you'd like to grow—with new positive ones.

Here are some examples of how to override negative thoughts when they pop up:

¤ **"I'm not good enough."** Is it true? Is it fact? Is it helpful? No. Override it with the truth by declaring, "I am
enough."

¤ **"I'm failing as a mom."** Is it true? Is it fact? Is it helpful?
No. Override it with the truth by declaring, "My child
doesn't need a perfect mom. My child needs a loving and
present mom. I am a loving and present mom. I'm the
mom my child needs."

¤ **"I don't fit in. People don't like me."** Is it true? Is it fact?
Is it helpful? No. Override it with the truth by declaring,
"I do fit in. I have immense value and incredible worth."

Treat your mind like a radio station. Why let it drone negativity
when you could be bopping to some summer jams that kids on
TikTok are dancing to? Okay, so move your elbows—nope, you're
doing the Carlton. There you go. Now you're getting it!

What's one negative thing you've been saying about yourself?
Override it. Ask yourself, "Is it true? Is it fact? Is it helpful?" Write
a positive declaration to replace it—and post this positive thought
where you'll see it regularly.

Your old thought-seeds of insecurity will be strong at first and
try to pull you back into the weeds. This is where you must tend to
the garden. You must nurture the new seeds so they have the time
to take root and grow—just like that Asian bamboo plant. Give
your new positive thought-seed some time and care. You can nurture—and strengthen—the new thought by repeating the positive
declaration.

After you've overridden a negative thought, then just as you
looked for ways to prove that your negative thoughts were correct, now you're going to look for ways to prove that your positive
thoughts are correct. This requires you to adjust your focus.

Train Your Thinking—Adjust Your Focus

Adjusting your focus is about looking at the bigger picture. When
we narrow in on what's wrong in our lives, what's wrong can end up

being all we see. Adjusting your focus is about stepping back and choosing to see what is good, what is right, and what is lovely. Here are a few examples of how you can step back and adjust your focus to see the positives:

- "I choose to focus on the best in others instead of the worst."
- "I choose to focus on the best in myself instead of perceived flaws."
- "I choose to focus on what might go right instead of what might go wrong."
- "I choose to focus on my successes instead of my failures."
- "I choose to focus on possibilities instead of limitations."
- "I choose to focus on being curious instead of being critical."
- "I choose to focus on all that I have instead of all that I've lost."

What is the most negative situation in your life right now? Can you think of something? Now adjust your focus. Focus on what is good, what is right, and what is lovely and list three positives about this same situation. It's okay if it takes some time. That's natural. It takes practice. It's like learning to ride a bike. You may have to start with training wheels. It might feel a little bumpy, a little wobbly, and a little unusual at first, and it might take a great deal of effort and concentration. You might even fall off your bike. But as you keep honing your skills, the training wheels will be off before you know it, and you'll be riding freely around town without giving it much thought. "Look, Mom, no hands!"

Note that if you are truly unable to see any positives about your situation, that may be a sign that you're experiencing depression, so please reach out to your physician or your therapist. When I went through a bout of depression, it was so very challenging to see the positives. With help, I was able to turn that all around. You can too!

Create Positive Outcomes with a Positive Mindset

The effort it takes to change your thoughts is worth it. Choosing a positive mindset will transform outcomes in *all* areas of your life. Think of it this way: A tomato seed, when planted, takes root. The root grows, a plant bursts through the soil, and eventually that plant produces a tomato. A thought-seed, when reinforced with reflection and repetition, takes root. It grows and becomes part of the neural network of your mind. That thought-seed generates a feeling. The feeling leads to action. Action leads to outcomes.

> A thought-seed, when reinforced with reflection and repetition, takes root. It grows and becomes part of the neural network of your mind. That thought-seed generates a feeling. The feeling leads to action. Action leads to outcomes.

Here's an example of how thoughts lead to feelings, which lead to actions, which lead to outcomes. Suppose you've joined a parenting group, and you find yourself thinking, *I don't belong. I don't fit in. They don't like me.* It's possible that something you've heard or seen has triggered a seed of insecurity for you, a thought which connected with other stored memories of times when you felt that *I don't belong. I don't fit in. They don't like me.* That's why your current thought feels so true. It's coming from a deep-seated memory. However, no matter how true something feels, that feeling doesn't make it true. Remember, feelings are not facts.

Suppose you don't override the negative thought. Suppose you accept it as true without challenging it. If you feel like you don't belong and that the others in the group don't like you, it might prevent you from talking to the other parents. This could trigger their own insecurities and cause them to believe it's *you* who doesn't like *them*. Their actions, stemming from their insecurities, might reinforce your incorrect belief. If you continue to believe the worst, you might drop out of the parenting group, believing you were right about not belonging, fitting in, or being liked. That negative thought has produced a negative outcome in your life: you missed out on the benefits of the parenting group. In addition, the limiting belief about yourself has been reinforced and has grown even stronger in the process.

For better outcomes, think better thoughts. Adjust your focus. Focus on the times you felt accepted, wanted, and loved. Focus on your value, not on your perceived flaws. Replace the old seeds of insecurity with new, nurturing truths. Here's what that would look like in the same scenario:

You're at the parenting group, and you think, *I don't belong. I don't fit in. They don't like me.* This time you choose to override the thought. You ask yourself, "Is it true? Is it fact? Is it helpful? No! I do belong here. I have immense value and incredible worth." This time, you also choose to adjust your focus: "I choose to focus on the ways in which I can contribute to this group. I choose to focus on the ways in which I can be a good friend to others. I choose to focus on all of the times I have felt accepted, loved, and valued in the past."

These kinds of thoughts lead to positive feelings, which can lead to positive actions and positive outcomes. Think about it. With that mindset, you're far more likely to build friendships and remain in the parenting group! Sure, Friday nights with your partner is fun, but hanging out with people your age who want to discuss the, ahem, appeal of *Bridgerton*—well, that will get the serotonin and dopamine balancing in your brain in no time!

Can you see how fixing the things you say to yourself impacts your attitude? It's much easier to choose an attitude of confidence when you're thinking confident thoughts. It's much easier to have an attitude of gratitude when you're thinking thankful thoughts. It's much easier to have a winning attitude when you're thinking winning thoughts.

As you continue to focus on what is good, what is lovely, and what is right, those positive thoughts become stronger. Over time, something amazing happens. Situations that once sparked your insecurity will lose their grip on you. You'll notice that your self-talk becomes more nurturing and encouraging and that it happens more automatically and with less effort.

What you've learned in this chapter is to let go of a deflated and defeated mentality. Thoughts are only thoughts, and thoughts can be changed. That change begins with a choice. Decide today to create a new mindset for yourself: make a decision to choose a positive attitude daily, and train your thinking by overriding negative thoughts and adjusting your focus to see what is good, what is right, and what is lovely. Your new positive mindset will generate a winning attitude, and more positive outcomes will show up in every area of your life.

Take a Break—Crossword Puzzle

Okay, Mama Bear, time for a break. This challenge will help you to reinforce what you've learned about thoughts and mindsets in this chapter.

(If you get stuck or are short on time, the answers are in the Notes at the back of the book.)[28]

Across:

3. A positive mindset creates positive _____.

4. To grow positive feelings, you must _____ positive thoughts.

5. Your thoughts are neurons, chemicals, and _____ impulses.

7. Adopting a positive attitude begins with a _____ and then continues by training.

Down:

1. As you're consciously choosing to think new thoughts, both the old and new thoughts will _____ for a time before the old one dies off.

2. Simply put: Your mindset is your established set of _____.

4. Adjusting your focus is about looking at the bigger _____.

6. Feelings are not _____.

CHAPTER 18

Take Control of Your Thoughts

The Five-Point Path

Picture this: it's a beautiful day. You wake up feeling positive about life. You even get out of bed extra early to indulge in some reading while sipping on your favorite morning beverage before the family wakes up. Your thoughts are in the right place. You get the kids off to school, and you're feeling pretty darn great!

Suddenly, one negative thought enters your mind, and BAM! You go from peace to panic in the blink of an eye. *What the heck happened?* Well, my friend, you just allowed your thoughts to control you. But today is the day you take back control of your thought-life. In just a moment, I'm going to hand you the five-point path to take control of your thoughts so that your thoughts don't control you. First, you need to know something pretty incredible about the way your brain works.

Did you know that when a thought first enters your mind, you have a mere twenty-four to forty-eight hours to change that thought? That's a faster turnaround than discovering a new slang word and then finding out that Gen Z has already stopped saying it. Pretty "cheugy" if you ask me.

In her book *Who Switched Off My Brain?*, Dr. Caroline Leaf explains it this way:

> *Electrical information created by your thoughts and exist-ing memories brought into consciousness whoosh through the hippocampus, moving toward the front of the brain (the basal forebrain, which is behind the inside corners of your eyes). The information stays in the hippocampus for 24 to 48 hours constantly being amplified each time it swirls to the front.*
>
> *This amplification means the thought is very conscious and becomes "labile" or unstable, which means it is moldable and can be changed. In fact, it must change. The science of thought demands that change must occur—either reinforc-ing the thought as it is or changing some or all of it.*[29]

In other words, when a thought first enters your mind, you can either dwell on it and make it stronger or you can use that window of time to reject the thought and replace it with a truth that builds you up, helps you to succeed, and gives you peace.

Here's an example of how I used this amplification process to my advantage. One day, I was dressed and ready to drive to the studio where I hosted a morning TV show. Both of my daughters had left for school, and the only thing I needed to do before driving to work was to take the trash out to the curb for collection. As I neared the end of my driveway, I tripped and fell. I hit the pave-ment so hard that my hands and knees started to bleed. I went back into the house and, feeling sorry for myself, began telling myself an entire story about how hard it was being a working mom and

> Your outer world is eventually going to look like what you've been telling yourself—either in secret or out loud—all day long. That's why you have to learn to take control of your thought-life!

how tired I was of having to do *everything*—like taking out the trash. These "poor me" thoughts overtook my mind, and I was just about ready to cry.

Then I paused and said to myself, "Denise, you have a choice. You can choose to continue feeling sorry for yourself, or you can choose to make today the best day you possibly can."

In that moment, I made a decision. I decided to have a great day instead of continuing to feel bad about something that was already over. As I drove to work, I declared out loud, "Today is going to be an amazing day, and nothing is going to get in my way. I am unstoppable. I'm going to have fun today. I may have fallen down, but I'm not staying down. I am already up and victorious! I love my life. I'm thankful for my amazing kids, and I am going to have the best day ever!"

My mood shifted significantly, and I had one of the best times I'd ever had hosting the show. I'm not exaggerating! I transformed my day by transforming my thoughts. My situation became a reflection of my self-talk. Yours will too! Your outer world is eventually going to look like what you've been telling yourself—either in secret or out loud—all day long. That's why you have to learn to take control of your thought-life!

But how? In the previous chapter, you learned how to plant new thought-seeds to override old thought-seeds of insecurity. You also learned how to nurture those new thoughts by choosing to adjust your focus. Here you'll build on that skill set by learning a five-point path for taking back control of your thoughts, so your thoughts won't control you—regardless of what happens in your day.

The Five-Point Path to Controlling Your Thoughts

First, let's look at what happens when your thoughts control you: A thought enters your mind, either from new information or stored memories. You focus on that thought, perhaps by dwelling on it, talking about it, or writing about it in a journal or maybe even on social media. By focusing on that thought, you reinforce it. The thought becomes stronger, and you become emotionally charged (negatively or positively) by it.

The thought is now in charge of your emotions. Yikes!

Now check out the sequence of events that occurs when you control your thoughts using the following five-point path:

1. **A thought enters your mind.** The thought comes from either from new information or stored memories.
2. **Decide to accept or reject the thought.** Ask yourself, "Is it true? Is it fact? Is it helpful?" If it is, keep it. If not, you can decide to reject it.
3. **Discover the truth.** If you've decided to reject that thought, ask yourself, "What is actually true?"
4. **Focus on the truth.** You can do this by thinking about the truth, writing it down, and/or speaking it out loud.
5. **Continue to focus on the new thought until the negative thought and the subsequent emotions dissipate.**

Notice that, in both cases, the very first thing that happens is a thought entering your mind. That is the only part of the path you can't control, but you can control what happens afterward. We can use the day I fell taking out the trash to see this five-point path in action:

1. **A thought enters your mind.** The one that entered my mind was "Poor me."
2. **Decide to accept or reject the thought.** I decided to reject it. I rejected it because it wasn't helpful. I certainly didn't want to feel that way. I also rejected it because it

was neither a fact nor the truth. I wasn't a victim. All that happened was that I fell down. I didn't have to create an entire story around it and make myself feel worse.

3. **Discover the truth.** I asked myself, "What is actually true?" I answered that question by saying, "Today is going to be an amazing day and nothing is going to get in my way. I am unstoppable. I'm going to have fun today. I may have fallen down, but I'm not staying down. I am already up and victorious! I love my life. I'm thankful for my amazing kids, and I am going to have the best day ever!"

4. **Focus on the truth.** I focused on that truth by speaking it out loud.

5. **Continue to focus on the new thought until the negative thought and the subsequent emotions dissipate.** I continued to speak that truth aloud on my drive to work, and soon I felt significantly better. The negative thoughts were gone. I took control of my thinking, and my entire day changed as a result.

Learning how to control your thoughts plays a significant part in helping you to stay—or get back to—calm. As we all know, things are going to happen in the course of the day, week, or year that could potentially throw you for a loop and leave you feeling completely stressed out. Sometimes those things will be small irritants: Your babysitter bails on you at the last minute, and you have to cancel date night. A stranger gives you her unsolicited two cents on your parenting skills. You leave the house with your kids and realize you forgot to pack the one and only thing you needed. As frustrating as these events can be, they are also wonderful opportunities to practice the five-point path to take control of your thoughts. Doing what you can to take control of your thoughts will help you master the art of not sweating the small stuff.

But what about the big stuff? Sometimes what happens in your life can be significant and painful: You get a bad health diagnosis. Your child gets hurt. You lose your job. When big stuff happens to you, take courage! The five-point path is designed to help you regain and maintain your inner peace—even during the big stuff.

A Case Study: How Jennifer Got Calm

Let me tell you another story, one about someone who used the five-point path to deal with some "big stuff" in her life. I've changed her name to Jennifer to protect her privacy, and I'm sharing this story with her permission.

At the time, Jennifer was a student of my online training course (which you can check out at calmonline.denisemarek.com). During one of our conversations as part of that course, Jennifer shared something with me: "I have a complex situation with my son and his wife. That's why I'm taking this course. I'm not a worrier actually. I'm fifty-two years old, and I've never been a worrier. Well, until three years ago, that is. The worry started after my son got married. Now my mind is in a constant state of stress."

She sighed and added, "Ugghh. Worry is draining!"

She explained that her son had gotten married at a very young age and that she felt his wife was hurtful and cruel to her and her family. Jennifer went on to tell me that, in reality, she didn't have any other people like her daughter-in-law in her life. She said, "At my age, I don't choose to have people in my life who are like that. You get to choose your friends and the people with whom you associate. At the first sign of her being such a mean person, I would have walked away. But she is married to my son, so I'm on the hook."

Jennifer's biggest worries were that she might lose her relationship with her son and his daughter (Jennifer's granddaughter). Those were big worries, and I really wanted to help her. So together, we looked at the action plan Jennifer had created using the second step of the CALM process: Act to Control the Controllable. That plan included the following:

- ¤ Find counseling and a support group for herself.
- ¤ Reduce relationship expectations and accept "what is."

¤ Make space for herself and set boundaries.

¤ Give the relationship with her son some time instead of chasing after it.

¤ Ask her son for weekly scheduled time to visit with her granddaughter.

Before Jennifer finished sharing her action plan, she stopped and looked up from her notes. She continued, "I have more actions written down, but I have to tell you something. I wrote a note to myself on my action plan, and it says, 'I had a plan before, and it failed over and over and over again. So now, I'm scared.'"

Of course she felt scared! This was new territory. She felt like her mother-child bond was being threatened, and that threat was signaling the stress response. (Remember learning about the stress response in Chapter 1? That time of fear and stress is precisely when you need to use the five-point path to regain control of your thinking!)

After validating Jennifer's feelings, I asked, "What is the difference between the action plan you created in the past and the new one you've created since learning about the CALM process?"

She quickly replied, "Reduce relationship expectations with my daughter-in-law." Then she added, "When I say I'm going to reduce expectations, I don't mean there won't be any relationship with my daughter-in-law. Maybe there will be at some point. However, I realize my expectations have been causing me a great deal of stress. I've been telling myself that I *should* have a close relationship with my daughter-in-law and my son's family. Who says that I *must* have a certain type of relationship with my daughter-in-law? Who's making that 'should'?"

Aha! Now we were uncovering the kingpin—or, in other words, the thought that was creating a logjam in Jennifer's thinking and robbing her of inner peace.

Now that you know Jennifer's situation, let's see how Jennifer applied the five-point path to her underlying belief system.

1. **A thought enters your mind.** Jennifer noticed this thought: "I should have a close relationship with my daughter-in-law."

2. **Decide to accept or reject the thought.** Jennifer decided to reject it. She had already decided to reject the "shoulds" and accept "what is" by altering her expectations of her relationship with her daughter-in-law.

3. **Discover the truth.** Jennifer is now in a position to discover the truth. Acknowledging the truth that nobody can force someone else to change, she can say, "I can succeed at setting healthy boundaries. I can continue to be a loving mom to my son and a loving grandmother to my granddaughter. I can remain open to a relationship with my daughter-in-law while keeping my expectations in check. I can succeed at following through on my new action plan."

4. **Focus on the truth.** Jennifer can speak out those new affirmations each time the old beliefs pop up.

5. **Continue to focus on the new thought until the negative thought and the subsequent emotions dissipate.** Jennifer continued to focus her thoughts on setting healthy boundaries, being a loving mother and grandmother, and remaining open to a relationship with her daughter-in-law while keeping her expectations in check. This ultimately helped her to reduce the stress and worry she had been feeling. By using the five-point path, Jennifer had taken back her inner peace.

After working through the first three steps of the CALM process and implementing this section of Master Your Mind, I asked Jennifer, "If you were to consider this situation not as happening *to* you but instead as happening *for* you, what do you think the possible benefits could be?"

She replied, "I really think that one day, I'm going to have to help somebody through the same situation. That's why I think this is happening. Maybe not with their daughter-in-law, but there's going to be a child involved, and it's going to be a behavior issue where someone is going to be feeling like me. I can see myself taking this painful experience and helping other people."

She then added, "Most of the time, people's deep growth doesn't happen through joyous events. They happen through tragedy, pain, and suffering. That's the water in the soil for the [thought-] seeds. That's how growth happens. You don't often hear people saying, 'I had this deep, meaningful, emotional growth on my relaxing vacation in the Caribbean.' They'll tell you, 'This terrible thing happened to me, and I walked through it, and I came out the other side with this knowledge and this depth.'"

That's what I call transformation! Did it change Jennifer's relationship with her daughter-in-law overnight? Of course not. However, it did change how she *felt* about that relationship. It gave her peace. And it gave her hope. Eventually, results will show up in Jennifer's outer world that reflect her new inner dialogue. Until that time, Jennifer has moved from being in a constant state of worry to taking back her inner peace.

How about you? Where do you need to take back control of your thinking? Start by paying attention to your thoughts. Maybe you're saying to yourself, "I'm just trying to make it through the day! Parenting is difficult; this should be easier. Life is hard, and I can barely handle it."

Change those thoughts now! Start affirming truths, such as "Of course I can handle this! I am strong! I am resourceful! I am capable of not just surviving but thriving! I will not be overcome because I am an overcomer."

Focus on these truthful thoughts until the negative thoughts and subsequent emotions dissipate. Making a consistent effort to implement this strategy will get you in the habit of letting go of that defeated and deflated mentality. When you take control of your thoughts, your thoughts will no longer be able to take control of you!

Take a Break—CALM Moms' Glad Libs

Now for some fun to reinforce what you've learned in this section. Complete the following list by filling in the blanks using the word prompts, or you can give the word prompts to someone else so their words will complete the story. You could even have someone else ask you the word prompts! (That way you aren't tempted to peek at the story ahead of time!)

If you have a child who's old enough, this would be a great game to play together. You could have some fun and then use this as a starting point for a discussion about how we can get emotionally charged by our thoughts. You can talk about the ways we can control those thoughts so they don't control us.

Okay, time to play!

- ¤ super-positive adjective_____
- ¤ your name_____
- ¤ any number_____
- ¤ any number_____
- ¤ negative emotion_____
- ¤ verb ending in "ing"_____
- ¤ fast-food restaurant_____
- ¤ noun_____
- ¤ plural noun_____
- ¤ noun_____
- ¤ your name_____
- ¤ positive adjective_____
- ¤ verb_____
- ¤ super-positive adjective_____
- ¤ noun_____
- ¤ verb ending in "ing"_____
- ¤ noun_____

¤ verb ending in "ing"_____

¤ noun_____

¤ same noun_____

¤ positive emotion_____

¤ body part_____

Now take the list of words you've created and use them to fill in the blanks in the following story:

Once upon a time, there was this [**super-positive adjective**] *mom named* [**your name**]. *She had* [**any number**] *children, all under the age of* [**any number**].

One day, she was feeling very [**negative emotion**]. *She had been* [**verb ending in "ing"**] *late several nights this week and was ordering* [**fast-food restaurant**] *for dinner again.*

"I should be a better [**noun**]," *she thought.*

In that moment, she realized her [**plural noun**] *were in control of her emotions. She decided to use the five-point path she learned in CALM for Moms to take back control of her thinking.*

1: A [**noun**] *enters your mind.* [**your name**]*'s distressing thought was, "I should be a* [**positive adjective**] *mom.*

2: Decide to [**verb**] *or reject the thought. This* [**super-positive adjective**] *mom knew she was doing the best she could and decided to reject the* [**noun**].

3: Discover the truth. "I am a [**verb ending in "ing"**], *caring, loving, and hard-working* [**noun**]," *she declared.*

4: Focus on the truth. In [**verb ending in "ing"**] *on the truth, she was able to see all of the things she was doing right.*

5: Continue to focus on the new [**noun**] *until the negative* [**same noun**] *and the subsequent emotions dissipate.*

Before she knew it, this mom felt [**positive emotion**] *again. With a* [**body part**] *filled with gratitude, she decided to stop "should-ing on" herself from now on.*

CHAPTER 19

Regulate Your Emotions

How to Stop Self-Sabotaging and End Emotional Suffering

Ever wonder why you didn't stick to your goals in the past—goals to lose weight, quit yelling at the kids, stop drinking, or whatever else it is you've been trying to achieve—even though you really, really, *really* wanted to? It might be because your current strategies for coping with worry and stress are in *direct conflict* with what you're trying to achieve. Stay with me here. Many of the things people do to make themselves feel better, like overeating, overspending, over-sedating, overmedicating—or even yelling at the kids—end up sabotaging the very thing they most want to achieve. So if your current strategies for coping with worry and stress are sabotaging the thing you most want to achieve, why do you keep doing it? It's because these unhealthy coping mechanisms provide *relief*.

The Truth about Alcohol

Let's use the coping mechanism of drinking alcohol as an example. It's so prevalent in our society that we've even coined a term for moms drinking alcohol to take the edge off parenting: "mommy wine culture." Be careful. Mommy wine culture is dangerous because it encourages the belief that you can't cope with your feelings. It makes light of alcoholism and increases the risk of alcohol abuse. Drinking to cope also compounds your problems because you've simply masked them rather than dealt with them.

By the way, if you feel like alcohol consumption has become a problem for you, kick any guilt or shame about asking for help to the curb. You can execute bold action and reach out to your health care provider or a local twelve-step program. Needing help with an addiction doesn't make you a bad mom. Getting help for an addiction makes you a courageous one!

Here's one of the hidden ways in which using alcohol for stress relief works against you. Scientific studies show that alcohol affects your sleep. It may give you a deep sleep at the beginning of the night, but there is a rebound effect. During the second half of the night, alcohol causes a fragmented, lighter sleep that is less restful.

Even slight sleep deprivation can affect memory, judgment, and mood. According to the American Psychological Association, "Many [adults] report that their stress increases when the length and quality of their sleep decreases. When they do not get enough sleep, 21 percent of adults report feeling more stressed. Adults with higher reported stress levels . . . fare even worse—45 percent feel even more stressed if they do not get enough sleep."[30] In essence, drinking alcohol to cope with stress could end up causing even greater stress.

Drinking alcohol has also been proven to make you eat more—without you even realizing it! The episode "Alcohol" in the documentary *The Truth About* shows a study in which two university sports teams joined an experiment that involved drinking beer.[31] The participants were told that the purpose of the experiment was to test how alcohol affects memory. In reality, the experiment sought to discover whether drinking alcohol makes you eat more. All participants in both groups were each given two pints of beer to drink, then bowls of snacks were placed in each group's room. However, unbeknownst to the participants, the control group's beer was *non-alcoholic*. The result? The group drinking the alcoholic beer consumed over three hundred calories more in snacks per person than the control group—and all without even noticing they were doing so. Can you see how much this coping strategy could backfire?

Because unhealthy coping mechanisms do provide relief, we often come back to them again and again when we feel stressed, despite the regret they inspire. Another good example of this is the stress-eating cycle.

The Stress-Eating Cycle—Why You Get Sucked In and How to Get Out

I'm using stress eating as an example, but you could easily substitute any unwanted habits you're trying to break, such as overspending, overmedicating, and so on. Is there a coping strategy you've been using for stress that's working against you? Keep that one in mind as we go through the typical stages of stress eating.

Okay, so you've committed (and recommitted) to sticking to your healthy-eating plan. But you feel stressed, overwhelmed, tired, frustrated with the kids, or even just bored, so you eat a donut, or a cupcake, or a cookie or two—or twelve. You feel relief—for a while. The relief wears off, and regret sets in. The regret triggers more stress, and you reach for those darn comfort foods again!

Why did it happen? You knew what you had planned to eat today. You promised yourself yesterday that today would be the day when you finally stick to your plan. You really, really wanted to achieve your goal. So why did incredible, smart, successful you stumble yet again?

Here it comes. I'm about to solve the mystery for you. It was because you were trying to avoid pain (such as stress) and/or gain pleasure (like eating tasty snacks). Let's take a look at how this pain/pleasure principle applies to the stress-eating cycle.

Stage 1: Stress

You stepped on a piece of Lego after you've repeatedly told the kids to clean it up. Your in-laws just texted to announce they're dropping by, even though you've specifically set boundaries to prevent surprise visits like this. You're looking at the mess you just tidied up yesterday and feeling frustrated that you have to keep cleaning up after other people. You feel stressed. When you feel stressed, your physical body will rise up to dull the pain—without any consideration of your long-term goals.

Stage 2: Indulge

In an attempt to dull the pain, you might start thinking about eating sugar or other addictive foods. (Feel free to insert your personal unwanted coping mechanism here.) While thinking about—or seeing—a comfort food you love, you're instinctively driven to eat it. From a survival perspective, eating it means life and not eating it means death!

On top of that, high-carb foods such as chocolate, pasta, bread, and so on are called *comfort* foods for a reason. Carbs boost the powerful brain chemical serotonin. Serotonin is a neurotransmitter that can help reduce depression and make you feel euphoric. (This certainly helps answer the question of why we might gravitate to eating processed carbs when we are worried and stressed!)

Combine this serotonin boost and your hard-wired survival response mechanism with the pain of stress, and the desire to eat kicks into high gear. It's no wonder the craving often wins. It's not a *failure* of willpower; it's the *strength* of your survival response at work. So you give into the craving and indulge by eating.

Stage 3: Relief

What happens while you're indulging? You feel relief. Sweet relief. Good, right? Not so fast, Mama Bear. While it's satisfying in the moment, the relief is temporary. Research shows that within only twenty minutes of eating processed carbs, any benefits dissipate. Once the relief fades, you soon discover that eating didn't help you avoid pain. Instead it created another kind of pain—the pain of regret.

Stage 4: Regret

When an emotion such as regret enters the mix, the desire to avoid pain gets magnified. Your body rises up again to dull the pain, and you find yourself trapped in a vicious cycle.

So there it is! The reason you stumbled, even though you really, really, *really* wanted to achieve your goal, was because you wanted to avoid pain and/or gain pleasure. And you're not alone.

The trouble is that a lot of the things people do to make themselves feel better (like drinking alcohol, spending money, taking drugs, or eating comfort foods) not only add fuel to the fire of stress and worry but they also provide only temporary relief. If eating comfort food only provides twenty minutes of comfort and consuming alcohol has you unknowingly eating more while also disturbing your sleep, would you consider trying a different way to get some relief?

If you said yes—and I hope you did—keep reading. You're about to learn how to regulate your emotions before you react in ways you may later regret.

The Eight-Action Sequence to Regulate Your Emotions

Implementing the strategies in this section will put you in a better position to stop self-sabotaging and end emotional suffering. Unlike some of the unhealthy ways of coping with worry that only offer temporary relief, following this eight-action sequence to regulate your emotions will provide you with longer-lasting relief in a much healthier way. You really *can* do this!

Let's face it: things happen over the course of your day that you just can't anticipate. Your child throws up on you just as you're heading out the door for work. Your little one throws a temper tantrum at the store. Your toddler refuses to get dressed. Your teenager is being extra moody and slams the door. For those emotionally charged moments, this eight-action sequence is a game-changer. By taking these actions, you'll be able to regulate your emotions and regain your inner peace before reacting in ways that you regret or that have you reaching for a temporary fix.

When you're emotionally charged, the urge to reach for those temporary fixes can be incredibly strong. But it's wise for you to regulate your emotions before reacting in the heat of the moment. You can do so by implementing the following eight-action sequence when you're feeling triggered. (To access a one-page printable summary of this sequence, visit www.denisemarek. com/endemotionalsuffering. Print it out and post it on your fridge, stick it on your bathroom mirror, or put it any other place where you'll see it at the moment you'll need it to remember to regulate your emotions *before* reacting.)

1—Pause

Pause and take a deep breath to calm your body, including your nervous system.

2—Observe the Emotion

Pay attention to how you're feeling by asking yourself these questions:

- ¤ "On a scale of 1 to 10 (1 = not very emotionally charged; 10 = extremely emotionally charged), how emotionally charged am I feeling right now?"
- ¤ "What emotion(s) do I feel right now?"

While you're observing your emotions, it's important to remember that you are not your emotion. Avoid describing emotions using "I am" language such as "I *am* sad" or "I am stressed." Instead, say, "I *feel* sad. I *feel* stressed."

3—Reflect on Your Reactions

Take some time to think about how these emotions have caused you to react in the past and how they are driving your current reactions. Ask yourself:

- ¤ "How have these emotions caused me to react in the past?"
- ¤ "Are my emotions driving my reactions, choices, and behaviors in this moment?"
- ¤ "What actions or responses are my emotions leading me to take right now?"

4—Uncover the Underlying Belief

Take a moment to expose the belief or thought triggering the emotion using the following four questions as prompts. While the last two questions are almost identical to the first two, the repetition is meant to prompt you to keep digging until you get to the underlying belief. Ask yourself:

- ¤ "What am I thinking or believing to be true, either about myself, the situation, or the world around me?"
- ¤ "If what I'm thinking or believing is true, what do I think it means about me? What do I think would happen as a result of it being true?"
- ¤ "What *else* am I thinking or believing to be true, either about myself, the situation, or the world around me?"
- ¤ "If *that* were true, what do I think it means about me? What do I think would happen as a result of it being true?"

5—Affirm the Truth

You have already been using this part of the sequence to replace faulty belief systems, override negative thoughts, and put an end to negative thinking. Use it to regulate your emotions too. Ask yourself:

- ¤ "Is that faulty belief true? Is it fact? Is it helpful?"
- ¤ "What is actually true?" Affirm the truth by thinking about it, writing it down, and/or speaking it out loud.

6—Accept the Emotion

Emotions are like waves; they ebb and flow, they come and go. Accept your feelings without trying to hold onto the ones you want to keep or force away ones you don't want. Remember, peace always returns. Affirm to yourself:

¤ "This too shall pass."

7—Choose Your Response

When choosing your response, keep in mind that sometimes no response is a good response. Ask yourself:

¤ "What do I feel is the best way to respond to the situation that triggered my emotions?"

8—Shift Your Focus to Gratitude

Focusing on things you're thankful for can improve your mood, leading to you feeling less emotionally charged. Ask yourself:

¤ "What three things am I thankful for?"

What are your biggest parenting triggers? Is it mealtime, your child's behavior, or their sleeping patterns? How do you normally respond when you're feeling triggered? Can you see yourself taking a deep breath *before* responding? Can you see yourself following this sequence of actions *before* reacting? Here's what it looks like when this sequence is put into action.

Emotions are like waves; they ebb and flow, they come and go. Accept your feelings without trying to hold onto the ones you want to keep or force away ones you don't want. Remember, peace always returns.

A Case Study: How Lindsay's and Brianna's Mom (Me) Found Her CALM

I found it! I thought, looking in the mirror. *It's the Mother-of-the-Bride dress of my dreams.*

My daughter Lindsay would be getting married in a few months—a huge deal in the life of a mom—and I had found *the* dress to wear for this momentous occasion. There was only one problem.

The salesperson—who reminded me of an energetic Salma Hayek—called to me from outside the fitting room. "How's it going in there?" she asked eagerly.

"I love it, but it doesn't fit," I replied.

Without warning, "Salma" tore open the white flowy curtain between us and confidently declared, "I can get you into that dress!" She had me suck in my stomach as much as humanly possible and use my hands to push in my ribcage while she struggled behind me with the zipper until finally—*ziiiiiiip.*

It zipped up! I thought. *It fits!*

(Oh, it fit alright. It fit just like the glass slipper on the stepsister's foot!)

I twirled around and around in my new dress with the biggest smile on my face. "This is the one," I said. "I'll take it." As I was paying for the dress, I said to the salesperson, "I'd like to lose a couple of pounds before the wedding. Will the dress still look okay if I do?"

She handed me back my credit card and said, "You can lose some weight, but you can't gain any."

Did I lose weight? Nope. In fact, lo and behold, over the summer I *gained* a few more pounds. Six weeks before the wedding, I couldn't get the dress zipped up. No matter how much I sucked in, pushed in, and struggled with that zipper, the dress would not zip up.

Okay, there's still six weeks before the wedding. It's fine. Breathe. You can just stick to a diet from now on, and it will be okay.

Two weeks after sticking to a strict diet, one which had worked for me in the past, I got on the scale.

What? I haven't lost any weight at all?

I slammed my bathroom door. (For the record, I'm not a door slammer by nature.) In that moment, I felt incredibly angry. I felt angry with myself. I felt angry with the scale. I felt angry with my body. Then I started to panic.

When you're feeling angry, triggered, panicked, upset, hurt, or broken-hearted, try using the eight-action sequence to regulate your emotions—before reacting in a way you may regret. Here's how I used the sequence when panic set in that day.

1—Pause

First, I took a deep, calming breath.

2—Observe the Emotion

Then, I paid attention to how I was feeling and observed my emotions by asking myself some questions:

- "On a scale of 1–10, how emotionally charged am I feeling right now?" *I would say I'm at level 10. My heart is pounding, and my thoughts are swirling.*
- "What emotion(s) do I feel right now?" *I am angry and I am afraid. Oh wait! I am not my emotion, so I'll rephrase that. I feel angry. I feel afraid.*

3—Reflect on Your Reactions

I took a moment to think about my past reactions to these emotions and how they were driving my current reactions:

- "How have these emotions caused me to react in the past?" *In the past, this out-of-control feeling has triggered me to succumb to eating disorders and extreme dieting.*
- "Are my emotions driving my reactions, choices, and behaviors in this moment?" *Yes. I've suddenly become a door slammer.*
- "What actions or responses are my emotions leading me to take right now?" *I'm pacing around the house like a lion*

and thinking about what I could eat to feel better, even though I know that binging comfort food won't ease my emotional suffering.

4—Uncover the Underlying Belief

Next, I did some digging to expose the underlying belief/thought triggering the emotions.

- ¤ "What am I thinking or believing to be true, either about myself, the situation, or the world around me?" *I have no control over my body.*
- ¤ "If what I'm thinking or believing is true, what do I think it means about me? What do I think would happen as a result of it being true?" *I'll never be able to lose weight, and I won't be able to fit into my Mother-of-the-Bride dress.*
- ¤ "What *else* am I thinking or believing to be true, either about myself, the situation, or the world around me?" *I'm unattractive and a failure.*
- ¤ "If *that* were true, what do I think it means about me? What do I think would happen as a result of it being true?" *I won't be wanted or loved.*

By this point, I was beginning to feel calmer. I was able to recognize that my panic and anger weren't really about the weight. Not fitting into the dress had triggered some past wounds (seeds of insecurity): When I was a kid, I had been bullied about my weight. The names others called me when I was growing up were so cruel that I had felt rejected, alone, and unworthy of love. My dress situation was causing the trauma I had experienced in my past to bubble to the surface. The emotional pain was an indication that I still had some mental and emotional wounds that needed healing.

Some of you reading this now have been made to feel a similar way. The harsh words of others have shaped your view of yourself. When people say things to you and about you long enough, you begin to believe that those things are true. When you have a view of yourself that has been shaped over time, or by stereotypes, or by previous generations, or by failures and past mistakes, there comes a point where you believe that's really who you are. The lies you've come to believe about your identity can become your prison. But you can walk right out of that prison once you know your true identity. Who you truly are is a person with immense value and incredible worth, and nothing you do—or don't do—can change that!

5—Affirm the Truth

After answering those questions and the beliefs underlying my emotions, I was now in a more positive frame of mind and in a better position to affirm the truth:

- ¤ "Is that faulty belief true? Is it fact? Is it helpful?" *No. It's not true. It's not a fact. It isn't helpful.*
- ¤ "What is actually true?" *The truth is that I am worthy, I am valuable, and I am loved. No number on the scale, type of dress I wear, or number of candles on my birthday cake can alter the truth about who I am.*

The same is true for you, Mama Bear. You're lovable, forgivable, wanted, accepted, and blessed. You're deserving and worthy. Those are magnificent truths to affirm! Affirming the truth will make an impression on your thoughts over time, and then your feelings will catch up with the new thoughts.

6—Accept the Emotion

After affirming the truth, I wasn't feeling angry or panicky anymore. I was feeling a little disappointed that I might have to find another dress for my daughter's wedding, and that's okay. My feelings—and your feelings—are valid. Of course I was feeling disappointed; I loved that dress, and I had been excited about it. It's okay to feel disappointed—or any other emotion, for that matter. It's okay to not feel okay. I accepted how I was feeling without trying to force the disappointment away. I reminded myself that peace always returns and I declared:

- ¤ "This too shall pass."

In the process of accepting your emotions, it's important to address and expose the Happiness Myth. This myth dictates that we're supposed to feel happy *all of the time* and that when we're feeling unhappy, it means something is wrong. This idea is simply incorrect.

Yes, being a mom is a gift. It's amazing. It's miraculous, breathtaking, and awe-inspiring. But it's also complicated, messy, heart-breaking, and challenging. That's why there are times you feel happy and times you feel sad. Times you feel blessed and times you feel stressed. Times you feel patient and times you feel impatient. There were times in those early years of parenting when I felt *like* a patient! "Doctor! I poured orange juice in my child's cereal and salt in my coffee. Oh, that's normal? I'm allowed to feel off on a Monday? I'm not a terrible person who should go to jail? Thanks."

Feel all the feels. And remember, emotions are like waves: they ebb and flow, they come and go. That's true for all of us. Accept your feelings without trying to hold onto ones you want to keep or force away ones you don't.

7—Choose Your Response

After following the first six actions in the sequence, it was time to choose my response. Keeping in mind that sometimes no response is a good response too, I answered another question:

¤ "What do I feel is the best way to respond to the situation that triggered my emotions?" *I'm no longer going to put myself through the anguish of extreme dieting to force myself into a dress that's too small. That desire was coming from a place of unresolved childhood trauma. Instead, I'm going to take the dress to my favorite tailor at Fernanda's Boutique and Alterations to see if she can adjust the seams to make the dress bigger. If that's not a possibility, I'll buy a new dress that fits for the wedding.*

8—Shift Your Focus to Gratitude

Lastly, I chose to improve my mood by thinking about things I'm grateful for.

¤ "What three things am I thankful for?" *I am thankful my daughter is getting married to a wonderful, caring man who loves her deeply. I am thankful to be the Mother of the Bride and that I have the chance to watch my baby walk down the aisle. I'm thankful I have the financial ability to alter the dress or to buy a new one.*

By the time I drove to the tailor's shop, I was at peace with my choices. This dress would be made bigger, or I would purchase a new dress for the wedding. I no longer felt the need to resort to old eating habits or to beat myself up for my perceived flaws. Fernanda asked me to try on the dress to determine if there was anything she could do. In one last attempt, she tried to zip me up.

"I can't zip this up," she said. "But I can let it out. There's enough extra fabric in the seams. You won't even be able to see that it's been adjusted." And she did. She masterfully altered the dress, and it fit me just right. I had thought it was my body that was all wrong. It turns out it was my belief system all along.

Can you see how working through these eight actions can take you from panic to peace? Can you see how you might use them to move from anger to calm before you say something you can't take back? Can you see how these actions can help you to make good choices out of love instead of fear or frustration?

After following the eight-action sequence, your emotions will be in a more moderate range. In this range, you're in a much better place to respond thoughtfully instead of reacting impulsively. Wise choices and actions come out of a moderate emotional range as opposed to an extremely high or an extremely low one.

Regulating your emotions and letting go of emotional suffering takes practice. However, with that practice, soon you'll be running laps around any suffering and hopping over negative thoughts like you're training for the mind-over-matter Olympics. Good thing it's only every four years.

CHAPTER 20

Tame Your Tongue

The Power of Your Voice Can Restore Inner Peace

One day, in Toronto, I was attending a seminar that a friend of mine was giving. When she was finished, I walked up to the front of the room to talk with her. A man from the audience also came up to speak with her. The three of us were standing there together when the man asked her, "How far along are you?"

She let him know that she was not pregnant. After the man walked away, she turned to me and, with a look of disbelief on her face, said, "That is the strangest pick-up line I have ever heard!"

How's that for taming your tongue? How would you have responded in that same situation? Would you have said something negative about your own appearance, about your outfit, or about the man? My friend did not speak out *one* negative word.

I had had something similar happen to me years earlier, but I wasn't as successful. Back in Chapter 14, I talked about a bout of mastitis I contracted a few days after my daughter Lindsay was born. A couple of weeks after that, I returned to the hospital by myself for a follow-up ultrasound appointment. My grandmother had offered to look after my new daughter for me. She came early, which gave me the opportunity to get showered and dressed up for my very first baby-free trip outside the house since the birth of my daughter.

I arrived at the hospital, and an orderly walked past me in the lobby. I recognized him as the man who had wheeled me around the hospital during the two failed attempts to induce labor. "Hey," he said. "I see you haven't had the baby yet."

Ugh! I wanted to disappear. I pretended I didn't hear him, and I walked in the opposite direction. I'd been feeling pretty good about myself until he said that. His comment had triggered a seed of insecurity in my mind. At that time, I didn't understand the power of thoughts and how to control them. If I had known then what I know now, I would have been able to calm my emotions and transform my negative thinking with thoughts like *Of course I still have a tummy—I recently had a baby. This miraculous body of mine created the little baby that I love so much. I'm so thankful to be a mom.* These kinds of thoughts would have helped me to restore my inner peace.

Instead, I beat myself up all the way home from the hospital. Then, when my husband got home from work, I complained to him about all the things I disliked about my appearance—and I complained for a very long time. But it wasn't helpful.

When you talk—that is, complain—about all the things you don't like, or everything you think is missing, or all of the things you think are going wrong or not working, it's like taking a shovel and digging up all of those positive thought-seeds you've worked so hard to plant. The sound of your voice has incredible power over your subconscious mind. Your mind will believe what it hears you saying more than it believes anyone else. The sound of your own voice magnifies and strengthens the thoughts you're thinking. Your words will make an impression on your subconscious mind—and they will eventually win out.

Your words have incredible power. You can use the power of your own voice to restore inner peace. To do this, *tame your tongue*. Taming your tongue means speaking positive words about yourself, others, your situation, and your life in general. It also means not speaking negative words about yourself, others, your situation, and your life in general. While you're not always able to choose what thoughts enter your mind, you can choose the words you use.

Mama Bear, it's not easy. However, it is doable—and *you* can do it! Here are some strategies to help you tame your tongue. Let's start by catching and correcting throwaway words.

Catch and Correct "Throwaway" Words— The Littles are Listening!

"I'm so tired," I said out loud with a big sigh as I drove home in my bright red Chevy Cavalier on a gloomy Tuesday afternoon.

Suddenly, a little voice from the back seat jolted me out of my thinking. The little voice said, "No, you're not, Mom. You're energized and refreshed!"

Lost in thought, I had momentarily forgotten that my chicklets were in the back seat. Be careful, Mama Bear; your littles are listening!

That little voice belonged to my daughter Lindsay. She was nine years old. I'd been teaching my kids to be mindful of the things they affirmed and declared out loud. Now they were catching me on my own slip-ups.

I looked at her little face in the rear-view mirror and said, "Good catch, Lindsay! I'm feeling more energized and refreshed already!"

This is how to tame your tongue. You catch and correct wrong thinking by paying attention to the words you speak out loud.

Understand, I'm not suggesting that you invalidate or ignore your feelings. It's important to acknowledge your feelings, check in with your needs, and take care of yourself. It's wise to talk with a therapist or a good friend about how you're feeling in order to get some help, find some peace, brainstorm possible actions, or help another parent to see that they're not alone in their own feelings. That kind of talk is helpful, positive, and necessary. By all means, be honest about how you're feeling.

What I'm talking about here is being on guard for "throwaway" words. These are words and statements said out of habit—even though they are in direct conflict with the thoughts, feelings, and outcomes you want showing up in your life. I'm talking about words like this: "I'm such a worrier." "I hate my car." "I'm so tired." Following the logic of Marie Kondo, does the negative thing you're saying spark joy? No? Then fold it into triangles, roll it to the street, and get it out of your life. (But I'll let you keep more than thirty books.)

When I said "I'm so tired" out loud in the car, I wasn't actually that tired. It was just one of those throwaway things I would say when I felt a little sluggish—like I did on that gloomy day. It was becoming a bad habit. By declaring "I'm feeling more energized and refreshed already" out loud, I triggered different thoughts and memories within myself. As a result, I actually started to feel more energized and refreshed.

You can tell a great deal about a person's thought-life by the words they use. Words are a reflection of what we think and believe. Too often, we just throw them around without giving their power much consideration. The words you use—whether positive or negative—are actually life-impacting affirmations.

Simply put, affirmations are declarations. When you say, "I'm going to enjoy today! I'm thankful! There are so many opportunities available, and they're coming my way," those are affirmations. When you say, "Nothing ever seems to go right. I'm such a worrywart. I'm never going to get ahead financially," those are all affirmations too.

What negative phrases do you habitually say out loud? Start paying attention to your own throwaway words. They will come up, and when they do, think of them as glorious opportunities. They indicate where negative thinking is at work in your subconscious mind. Once you're aware of your throwaway words, you have the opportunity to change them. By changing them, you are no longer allowing them to quietly run the programming of your mind behind the scenes. How awesome is that?

How about acknowledging how you feel, taking action to address your needs—and then saying some positive things about yourself too! What are some of the more positive "I am" statements you could say out loud? Here are some to consider:

I am confident.

I am more than a conqueror.

I am loved.

I am an overcomer.

I am protected.

I am blessed.

I am forgiven.

I am accepted.

I am victorious.

I am a visionary.

I am free.

I am filled with a spirit of thanksgiving.

I am fearfully and wonderfully made.

I am prosperous.

I am successful.

I am talented.

I am healthy.

I am energetic.

I am strong.

I am generous.

I am valuable.

I am resourceful.

I am capable of not just surviving but thriving!

When you begin declaring truthful positive affirmations about your life, your negative thoughts lose their grip on you. Thoughts, even habitual thoughts, can be changed. Affirm the positive to help build a new thought-life—to renew your mind. It will have a significant impact on the outcomes you're getting in every area of your life!

But what if these outcomes are taking too long? If that thought starts creeping in, it's time to mind the gap.

Mind the Gap: Declare Victory to Overcome Doubt

"Mind the gap" is a phrase used to warn train passengers of the chasm that exists between the train and the station platform. To get safely on and off the train, passengers must be mindful of that space.

To continue to nurture the new, positive thought-seeds you've worked so hard to plant, you too must mind the gap. Only this time, the gap isn't the place between the train and the station platform. This gap is the place that exists between the place you are now and the place you want to be.

It's so easy to keep positive at the beginning of something. You're full of hope and excitement. Your positive thinking leads to emotions that fuel positive behaviors and outcomes. Then one day you feel like it's taking longer than you thought it would. It's taking longer than you think it *should*.

> Resist digging up in doubt what you planted in faith. Trust that the process is working even when you don't see immediate results. Victory is coming your way!

You start wondering, "Hey, wait. I've been thinking positive thoughts. I've been using the eight-action sequence to regulate my emotions, and it's not working. It's taking too long. I'm giving up. Nothing ever works out for me."

That's the danger of the gap. Doubt resides in the gap. Doubt can cause you to speak negative words about your situation. It can cause you to dig up those positive thought-seeds you planted.

What you need is some faith to last you through the middle. Resist digging up in doubt what you planted in faith. Trust that the process is working even when you don't see immediate results. Victory is coming your way! All day long, declare, "I am blessed. I am victorious. I am prepared. I am qualified." Use the power of "I am," and doubt can no longer defeat you.

Let me paraphrase a statement by Carl Jung: "You're not what you say you are; but what you say, you are." When you speak positive words about your life, something amazing happens. Just as you looked for ways to prove you were right about the negative thoughts, you'll look for ways to prove you're right about the positive ones. As a result, what you tell yourself you are, you will become. Only this time, what you'll become is a more peaceful, more powerful, and more thankful you.

Walk by Faith, Not by Sight

Margaret Marek knew a thing or two about declaring victory over her life. Margaret became a first-time mom at the age of ninety-three. Whoa! I thought I'd waited a long time for some of my dreams to happen.

How does a ninety-three-year-old woman become a first-time mom? Well, at the age of ninety-three, Margaret married Mel, an eighty-nine-year-old widower. On the day they were married, Margaret became a (step)mom to Mel's two grown sons and a grandmother to his four grandchildren—which included my two daughters, Lindsay and Brianna.

Margaret's new sons and grandchildren visited and called her and Mel frequently. They sent Margaret flowers and cards every Mother's Day. Before passing away—three months before her hundredth birthday—Margaret experienced being a mother for seven years!

Is there something you've been wanting that hasn't yet happened? When there's something you really want and it's out of your reach, it's natural to feel disappointed.

John C. Maxwell said, "Disappointment is the gap that exists between expectation and reality."[32] During that gap, you have a choice. You can allow the disappointment to dominate your life—and your language—or you can choose to walk by faith, not by sight.

Walking by faith isn't necessarily about religion—though it can be. It's about choosing to remain hopeful and confident and to trust that good things are possible for you, your child, and your life—regardless of how things appear.

Walking by sight, on the other hand, is about relying solely on what you can see. This can become a dream destroyer, a hope drainer, and a worry maker. When you rely solely on what you see—especially when what you see isn't what you want—disappointment can turn into fear. You may begin saying things like "What if I don't have what it takes? What if it's too late? What if it never happens?"

How do you walk by faith when you're in the gap between expectation and reality? Use the tools you've learned so far in this chapter. First, resist talking about what you dislike in your current situation; that can be an easy way to get and stay stuck. Next, use positive declarations. All day long, remind yourself, "It's not too late. Anything is possible for my life!"

Anything is possible for your life! Yes, there are certain limitations we must all deal with—sometimes things happen beyond our control. However, often what we perceive as limitations are simply old or faulty belief systems and wrong thinking that are tripping us up. These limitations can absolutely be removed. Don't allow your sight to shake your faith.

Take a leap! Just like all leaps of faith, it's best done with a running start and a loud "AHHHHHHHH!" You've got this, Mama Bear!

Take a Break—Tongue-Taming Time

What have you been saying you are? What do you believe are the most important "throwaway" words for you to replace? Write them down, along with any negative phrases you habitually say out loud. Next, write down some positive "I am" statements you'd prefer to use instead in the future.

If your littles are old enough, consider enlisting them to help you to tame your tongue, mind the gap, and walk by faith by creating a *Can't Say "Can't"* jar. Every time they catch you (or you catch yourself) saying something from your "throwaway" words list, put a pre-determined amount of money in the jar while saying aloud your preferred positive "I am" statement. When there is enough saved, take your littles and yourself out for a treat to celebrate.

Yes, Mama Bear, it's a celebration! You're doing the work to catch and replace negative thinking, and that deserves recognition. You'll also be teaching your children the importance of managing the things they say within their own minds. They too will become what they say they are. By learning how to master their minds now, what they will become are self-assured, more joyful, confident adults.

Look at you, Mama Bear! You've learned some incredible strategies to master your mind. You know how to choose your mindset. You've discovered the way to take back control of your thoughts. You're equipped with the eight-action sequence to regulate your emotions. You know what to do to tame your tongue. You did the work, and I'm giving you a standing ovation! (I literally just stopped writing and stood up to applaud you! I really did!)

Now it's time for you to move to the final chapter in this book, where you'll find your Transformation Tracking Sheets. These sheets put the entire CALM process together in one place. All of the steps and strategies you've just learned are assembled in this "at-a-glance" format to make it easy for you to apply the four-step CALM process—and to continue enjoying your new worry-free life!

PART 5

Put It All Together

One worry at a time, one step at a time,
the CALM process will ease your worried mind.

How does a child learn to walk? One step at a time. The same is true when it comes to transforming worry into inner peace. One worry at a time, one step at a time, the CALM process will ease your worried mind. To assist you, in this section you'll find Transformation Tracking Sheets.

These sheets put the entire CALM process together, in one place, to provide you with your own personal—at-a-glance—template for worry-free living. You can use these Transformation Tracking Sheets in two ways:

One, when a worry comes up for you, you can start at the beginning and answer the first question: *What am I worried about?* Then, work your way through the steps by answering the questions and/or using the prompts as you go along.

Two, you can go immediately to the section you need most. For instance, if you're feeling emotionally triggered, you might want to hop to the strategies in the section Master Your Mind. If you need help crafting your action plan, you might want to skip on over to that section for ideas and strategies to help you. If your imagination is assuming the worst, jump straight to Challenge Your Assumptions. You get the picture.

Mama Bear, make sure to check in with these pages often. Use them as a guide to help you maintain inner peace today and keep worry away.

CHAPTER 21

Transformation Tracking Sheets

Your Personal Template for Worry-Free Living

To restore CALM, challenge your assumptions, act to control the controllable, let go of the uncontrollable, and master your mind.

¤ *What am I worried about?*

STEP 1: C = CHALLENGE YOUR ASSUMPTIONS

¤ *What assumption(s) am I making? Am I in physical danger?* If your answer is yes, you'd likely already be taking action to protect yourself. Your stress response would guarantee it. If your answer is no, take a few deep, calming breaths and redirect your thoughts to the present using the strategies provided in Chapter 1. Acknowledge you're not in physical danger by affirming, "I am safe. I am not in physical danger."

¤ *Is it true? Is it fact? Is it helpful?* Test your thoughts using these three questions from Chapter 2. Answering these questions will help you to stop granting negative assumptions an all-access pass to your mind.

¤ *HALT! Am I hungry, angry, lonely, or tired?* If you're experiencing even one of those symptoms, recognize that they are likely causing your assumptions to take a downward turn. Follow the suggestions outlined in Chapter 3 to remedy your needs.

¤ *On a scale of 1 to 10, how probable is it that what I'm worried about will happen?* When answering this question (from Chapter 4), did you rate your worry a 5 or less? This low rating on the scale of probability is a fair indication that what you're worried about isn't going to happen. Did you rate your worry a 9 or less? Keep calm, because there's still a good chance that what you're worried about is not going to occur. Did you rate your worry a 10? Take a deep breath, because there's hope! The next three steps in the CALM process will help you let go of worry—even those worries with a 10 rating!

¤ *Am I engaging in "what-if" thinking?* Try these three cures (from Chapter 5): Ask yourself, "What is?" Ask yourself, "Will it matter a year from now?" Affirm to yourself, "I'm capable of handling it—and my kids are too!"

¤ *What else could it be?* This question is meant to help you rewrite the story you tell yourself by focusing on a positive explanation in that time between the first inkling of worry and the relief of getting the facts. At times, your emotions can be triggered so quickly and be so overpowering that you may have a difficult time recognizing how you ended up feeling the way you do. When that happens, try the following suggestions (from Chapter 6) to help you organize your thoughts and restore your inner peace:

» Identify the worry-trigger. Ask yourself, "What did I see, hear, or read that triggered my current worry or fear?"

» Identify your scary thoughts. Ask yourself, "What is my scary story?"

» Start seeking out the facts. Ask yourself, "What actually happened or is happening?"

» Fill in the missing pieces with positive assumptions. Ask yourself, "What else could it be?"

STEP 2: A = ACT TO CONTROL THE CONTROLLABLE

¤ *Is this worry prompting me to take action?* If yes, create a written action plan using the following prompts:

> » *Who could I ask? What could I do? What could I read?* Using your answers to those questions (from Chapter 7), take five or ten minutes right now to craft a written action plan. It's not necessary for you to answer these questions in order or even have answers for each question. They are simply prompts to guide you to possible actions you could take. Write down your answers to those three questions as they come. Remember to write it on paper, think big, and be creative.

¤ *Is the fear of rejection stopping me from taking action?* To overcome the fear of rejection, avoid taking it personally (as outlined in Chapter 8.).

¤ *Is worrying about what other people think stopping me from taking action?* To let go of worrying about what other people think, choose to care more about what you think of yourself (as outlined in Chapter 8).

¤ *Is fear of criticism stopping me from taking action?* To let go of the fear of criticism, consider the source (as outlined in Chapter 8).

¤ *Is self-doubt stopping me from taking action?* To let go of self-doubt, focus on what you can do (as outlined in Chapter 8).

¤ *What actions can I take to reduce the physical and emotional effects of stress and worry?* Use one or more of the following "doable dozen" for Mama Bear's self-care (from Chapter 9):

> » Reduce noise triggers. Ask yourself, "Where can I turn down the volume in my environment today?"

> » Nurture yourself in nature. Ask yourself, "How am I getting outside today?"

» Reduce mess triggers. Ask yourself, "What three items of clutter can I decide today to discard, donate, recycle, or sell?"

» Tickle your funny bone. Ask yourself, "How can I add laughter to my day today?"

» "Run away" from worry. Ask yourself, "How can I move my body today?"

» Accomplish one small task. Ask yourself, "Have I made my bed today?"

» Develop your spiritual life. Ask yourself, "What is one worry I will pray about today?"

» Boost serotonin. Ask yourself, "Who will I extend kindness to today?"

» Overcome "request for help" triggers. Ask yourself, "What do I need help with today? Who could I ask to help me?"

» Practice gratitude. Ask yourself, "What three things am I thankful for today? What made today great?"

» Simplify your life. Ask yourself, "What on my to-do list can I let go of today?"

» Manage your commitments. Ask yourself, "Would I benefit physically, emotionally, or mentally from saying no to some requests today?"

¤ *Is there a bold action I've been putting off or avoiding because it feels too scary or too difficult to do?* If so, use the following suggestions (from Chapter 10) to help you make value-based decisions and take courageous steps forward on those values:

» Identify your values. Ask yourself, "What gives my life meaning and purpose? What is important to me? What brings me the most joy?"

» Check your decisions against your values. Try the decision-making tool from Chapter 10. After doing so, if you decide this particular bold action is in alignment with your values, I encourage you to take action today because of what you will become: a more fulfilled, more courageous, happier you!

STEP 3: L = LET GO OF THE UNCONTROLLABLE

¤ *Am I worrying about something over which I have no control?* If you are, use the suggestions provided in this step of the CALM process to help you to let go of the uncontrollable.

¤ *Am I feeling upset or sorry for myself about something that happened in the recent or distant past?* If yes, let go of upset feelings by following these prompts:

» Validate your feelings. Pay attention to how you're truly feeling, acknowledge your feelings, and tell yourself, "It's okay for me to feel the way I feel."

» Identify cognitive distortions. Ask yourself, "What story am I telling myself about what happened? Am I all-or-nothing amplifying, assuming, catastrophizing, discounting positives, making feelings facts, positive-blocking, or should-ing?" If you can answer yes to any of these, move to the next prompt.

» Flip the script. Replace your cognitive distortions with more accurate thoughts using the remedies provided in the stinkin' thinkin' list in Chapter 11.

¤ *Are there unresolved hurts from my past?* If yes, work through the following prompts (from Chapter 12) to let go through forgiveness:

» Ask yourself, "Who do I need to forgive? What did that person do or say to me that was hurtful? How did that experience make me feel? What did it make me believe about myself? Is that belief true? If not, what is true?"

» Declare, "I can choose to forgive," then craft your forgiveness statement:

"I choose to forgive [**the person's name**] *for* [**what was said or done**] *which made me feel* [**how you felt**] *and believe* [**what you believed**]. *I forgive myself for allowing* [**the person's name**] *to have the power to define my value, worth, or quality of life. I take that power away now through forgiveness."*

» Next, tear up your forgiveness statement and throw it away. Choose to declare, "I am difficult to offend. I am a forgiving person."

¤ *Am I feeling guilty?* If so, use the following recommendations (from Chapter 13) to let go of guilt:

» Eliminate the word "should." Ask yourself, "Is the word 'should' at the root of my guilty feelings?" If yes, challenge your beliefs by asking, "Is it true? Is it fact? Is it helpful?"

» Acknowledge that you're doing your best. Ask yourself, "Am I doing the best I can?" We are all doing the best we can with the tools and knowledge we have in the moment. You're doing your best, and your best is enough.

» Take appropriate action. Ask yourself, "Is what I'm doing appropriate in this situation?" If it is, acknowledge that fact to release guilt. If it's not, ask yourself, "What actions can I take to make positive changes?" Add those actions to your action plan and follow through.

» Be curious instead of self-critical. Instead of being critical ("I yelled at my child; I'm such a bad mom"), try being curious. Ask yourself, "What do I need right now?"

» Make amends. Ask yourself, "Do I need to make amends?" If so, apologize, take responsibility for your actions, and decide to modify future behavior.

» Learn from mistakes. Ask yourself, "What did I learn from this mistake, and what will I do differently next time?" The answers to this question will turn the "mistake" into something of value.

¤ *Have I entered the mom-shaming arena?* If so, follow these dos and don'ts (from Chapter 14) to let go of judgment:

» Don't comment on Mom's body shape or weight.

» Do encourage Mom with non-appearance-based compliments.

» Don't judge Mom for taking time for herself.

» Do support Mom's choice of self-care.

» Don't question Mom's child's development.

» Do acknowledge every child develops at a slightly different rate.

» Don't question Mom's parenting choices.

» Do recognize Mom is doing her best.

¤ *Am I feeling mom-shamed?* If you are, use the suggestions outlined in Chapter 14 to help you consider the source, care about what *you* think of yourself, look at the bigger picture, and stand your ground.

¤ *Is perfectionism eroding my inner peace?* If so, follow these suggestions from Chapter 15:

» Adjust your self-talk. Silence that inner voice that tells you that anything less than 100 percent isn't good enough. Refer to Chapter 15 for adjustments you can make to your self-talk.

» Aim for connection instead of perfection. Connection heals and perfection steals. Go ahead and connect with others now instead of waiting for things to be perfect.

» Think progress, not perfection. You are a work in progress. Be patient with yourself. When perfectionism tries to tear you down, think progress, not perfection.

» Accept "what is." Look up from your perceived flaws and shortcomings and accept "what is."

» Get comfortable making mistakes. To do that, try these three suggestions: Make more mistakes. Learn from your mistakes. Make decisions and take action in alignment with your values.

¤ *Do I need to let go of fear?* A remedy for fear is faith. After you have taken all the actions you can to control the controllable—when all that's left for you to do is let go—have faith. Refer to Chapter 16 for help choosing faith over fear.

STEP 4: M = MASTER YOUR MIND

¤ *Are negative thoughts contributing to my stress and worry?* If so, use the suggestions in this step of the CALM process to master your mind.

¤ *Am I feeling mentally or emotionally deflated?* There are times we can feel a little less confident, a little less optimistic, or a little less positive. These feelings are a normal part of life. It's okay for you to feel the way you do. However, it's important to understand that you don't have to stay deflated. Use the following strategies (from Chapter 17) to choose your mindset. These strategies will help you to override negative thoughts and create positive outcomes in your life.

> » Make the decision to choose a positive attitude daily. Ask yourself, "What is my desired attitude for today?" Refer to the list of examples of positive attitudes provided in Chapter 17.
>
> » Train your thinking—override the negative. Identify one negative thing you've been saying to yourself. Override it. Ask yourself, "Is it true? Is it fact? Is it helpful?" Write a positive declaration to replace it—and post this positive thought where you'll see it regularly.
>
> » Train your thinking—adjust your focus. Adjusting your focus is about looking at the bigger picture. When we narrow in on what's wrong in our lives, what's wrong can end up being all we see. To adjust your focus, step back and ask yourself, "What is good, what is right, and what is lovely?"

¤ *Do I need to take back control of my thinking?* If you do, take control of your thoughts using the five-point path as outlined in Chapter 18.

> » A thought enters your mind.
>
> » Decide to accept or reject the thought. Ask yourself, "Is it true? Is it fact? Is it helpful?" If it is, keep it. If not, you can decide to reject it.
>
> » Discover the truth. If you've decided to reject that thought, ask yourself, "What is actually true?"

» Focus on the truth. You can do this by thinking about the truth, writing it down, and/or speaking it out loud.

» Continue to focus on the new thought until the negative thought and the subsequent emotions dissipate.

¤ *Am I feeling emotionally charged right now?* Use this eight-action sequence (from Chapter 19) to regulate your emotions before reacting in ways that you regret or that have you reaching for a temporary fix:

» Pause. Take a deep breath to calm your body.

» Observe the emotion. Ask yourself:

• "On a scale of 1 to 10 (1 = not very emotionally charged; 10 = extremely emotionally charged), how emotionally charged am I feeling right now?"

• "What emotion(s) do I feel right now?" (When answering, use "I feel" language rather than "I am" language.)

» Reflect on your reactions. Ask yourself:

• "How have these emotions caused me to react in the past?"

• "Are my emotions driving my reactions, choices, and behaviors in this moment?"

• "What actions or responses are my emotions leading me to take right now?"

» Uncover the underlying belief. Ask yourself:

• "What am I thinking or believing to be true, either about myself, the situation, or the world around me?"

• "If what I'm thinking or believing is true, what do I think it means about me? What do I think would happen as a result of it being true?"

- Continue asking and answering these two questions until you feel like you've uncovered the underlying belief.
» Affirm the truth. Ask yourself:
  - "Is that faulty belief true? Is it fact? Is it helpful?"
  - "What is actually true?" Affirm the truth by thinking about it, writing it down, and/or speaking it out loud.
» Accept the emotion. Affirm to yourself:
  - "This too shall pass."
» Choose your response. Ask yourself:
  - "What do I feel is the best way to respond to the situation that triggered my emotions?"
» Shift your focus to gratitude. Ask yourself:
  - "What three things am I thankful for?"

¤ *Am I using my voice to speak out positive declarations about myself, my children, my family, my situation, and my life? Are there any areas in which I need to tame my tongue?* Use the power of your voice to restore inner peace by practicing these tips from Chapter 20.
  » Catch and correct "throwaway" words. Pay attention to the words you speak out loud. Replace negative declarations with more positive "I am" statements such as these: "I am strong. I am victorious. I am loved."
  » Mind the gap: declare victory to overcome doubt. The "gap" is the place that exists between the place you are now and the place you want to be. Doubt resides in the gap. Doubt can cause you to speak negative

words about your situation. Trust that the process is working even when you don't see immediate results. Declare, "I am blessed. I am prepared. I am qualified!"

» Walk by faith, not by sight. There are certain limitations we must all deal with—sometimes things happen beyond our control. However, often what we perceive as limitations are simply old or faulty belief systems and wrong thinking that are tripping us up. These limitations can absolutely be removed. Don't allow your sight to shake your faith. Speak out positive declarations such as "It's not too late. Anything is possible for my life!"

Dear Mama Bear,

You did it! Congratulations, Mama Bear—you've successfully completed the proven four-step CALM process to transform worry into inner peace! If this was a game of Monopoly, I'd tell you to go directly to the self-care bingo card in Chapter 9, highlight "Made progress toward my meaningful goal," and collect $200 for passing Go!

Bravo! You've acquired the skills to stop worrying. You've discovered strategies to challenge your assumptions and put an end to "what-if" thinking. You know how to take action to control the things you can and let go of the things you can't. You have the tools to master your mind in order to create positive outcomes, take control of your thoughts, regulate your emotions, and restore your inner peace. You now possess the skills, strategies, and steps to truly move forward in your life—calm, confident, and joy-filled.

Celebrate! What you've accomplished in completing this book is significant—for you and for your children. Your children will feel the ripple effect of the work you've just done. Using the steps to be a calm mom that you've learned here will help you to be happier, more present, and less stressed. It will help you to raise children who will grow up to be happier, more present, and less stressed too! That's a big deal.

Thank you! Thank you for allowing me to be a part of your parenting journey. I encourage you to continue using all of the tools you've just learned. Refer to this book, and these steps, again and again to nurture your newfound calm and regain your inner peace any time life throws you a curve ball or worry arises. Soon using the CALM process will become second nature for you and you'll be transforming worry into inner peace at record-breaking speeds!

Always know this: You are one strong Mama Bear! If inner strength was visible, you'd see six-pack abs and pickle-jar-opening biceps! You are smart and resourceful. You have immense value and incredible worth! You are enough. You belong. You are loved beyond measure and more treasured than you can imagine.

Love,

Denise

NOTES

1. L. R. Knost, Facebook post, April 24, 2017, https://www.facebook.com/littleheartsbooks/photos/when-little-people-are-overwhelmed-by-big-emotions-its-our-job-to-share-our-calm/1449215911775675/.

2. Denise Marek, *CALM: A Proven Four-Step Process Designed Specifically for Women Who Worry* (Carlsbad, CA: Hay House, 2006).

3. Sanjay Gupta, *Keep Sharp: Build a Better Brain at Any Age* (New York: Simon and Schuster, 2021), 132.

4. *CALM Online* is an online training program (taught by Denise Marek) that teaches strategies to let go of worry, reduce stress, and create a happier life. To register for the course, visit https://calmonline.denisemarek.com

5. Bruce Aylward, https://www.ctvnews.ca/video?clipId=1762678, in Avery Haines, "Social distancing is the new norm as the world tries to contain COVID-19," CTV–W5, March 13, 2020, https://www.ctvnews.ca/w5/social-distancing-is-the-new-norm-as-the-world-tries-to-contain-covid-19-1.4850801.

6. *Letters to My Wonderful Mom Read Me When Box*, available at knockknockstuff.com/products/letters-to-mom-read-me-when-box. © Knock Knock LLC, 2016. Excerpt courtesy of Knock Knock LLC.

7. Tiffany Field, "Postpartum Anxiety Prevalence, Predictors and Effects on Child Development: A Review," *Journal of Psychiatry and Psychiatric Disorders*, vol. 1, no. 2 (2017): 86–102, https://www.fortunejournals.com/articles/postpartum-anxiety-prevalence-predictors-and-effects-on-child-development-a-review.pdf.

8. *The Five-Minute Journal*, Intelligent Change Inc., https://www.intelligentchange.com/products/the-five-minute-journal.

9. Jeff Herman and Deborah Levine Herman, *Write the Perfect Book Proposal: 10 That Sold and Why*, 2nd ed. (New York: Wiley, 2001).

10. *Ted Lasso*, season 1, episode 6, "Two Aces," featuring Jason Sudeikis, aired September 4, 2020.

11. Gupta, *Keep Sharp: Build a Better Brain at Any Age*.

12. William H. McRaven, *Make Your Bed: Little Things That Can Change Your Life . . . and Maybe the World* (New York: Grand Central Publishing, 2017), 110–12.

13. Caroline Leaf, *Who Switched Off My Brain? Controlling Toxic Thoughts and Emotions* (Nashville: Thomas Nelson, 2009), 115.

14. Jim Rohn, *The Treasury of Quotes* (Southlake, TX: Jim Rohn International, 2006), 98.

15. You can print off a list of close to four hundred values from www.denisemarek.com/valueslist.

16. "Yesterday, Today, and Tomorrow," *The AA Grapevine*, vol. 2, no. 2 (July 1945), https://www.aagrapevine.org/magazine/1945/jul/yesterday-today-and-tomorrow.

17. Zig Ziglar, "We All Need a Daily Check-Up," Ziglar.com, https://www.ziglar.com/quotes/we-all-need-a-daily-check-up-from/.

18. Walt Disney, "Why worry? If . . ." D23: The Official Disney Fan Club, https://d23.com/walt-disney-quote/page/5/.

19. Amber Mamian, "70 Funny Parenting Quotes That Sum Up Parenting to a Tee," Rookie Moms, November 30, 2021, https://www.rookiemoms.com/funny-parenting-quotes/.

20. Caroline Leaf, *Cleaning Up Your Mental Mess: 5 Simple, Scientifically Proven Steps to Reduce Anxiety, Stress, and Toxic Thinking* (Grand Rapids, MI: Baker Books, 2021), 262–63.

21. Sean Stephenson, *Get Off Your "But": How to End Self-Sabotage and Stand Up for Yourself* (San Francisco, CA: Jossey-Bass, 2009), 55.

22. Edward M. Hallowell, *Worry: Hope and Help for a Common Condition* (New York: Random House, 1997), xiv.

23. Vic Johnson, *Day by Day with James Allen* (Melrose, FL: Sylvia's Foundation, 2003), 59.

24. Zig Ziglar, "How High You Bounce," Ziglar.com, https://www.ziglar.com/quotes/its-not-how-far-you-fall/.

25. John C. Maxwell, *Make Today Count: The Secret of Your Success Is Determined by Your Daily Agenda* (New York: Center Street, 2004), 1.

26. Mac Anderson, *The Power of Attitude* (Nashville, TN: Countryman, 2004), 10.

27. The Free Dictionary, s.v. "permanent, adj.," https://www.thefreedictionary.com/permanent.

28. Crossword Puzzle answers: Across: 3. OUTCOMES. 4. PLANT. 5. ELECTRICAL. 7. CHOICE. Down: 1. COEXIST. 2. ATTITUDES. 4. PICTURE. 6. FACTS.

29. Leaf, *Who Switched Off My Brain?*, 59–60.

30. "Stress and Sleep," *American Psychological Association*, 2013, https://www.apa.org/news/press/releases/stress/2013/sleep#:~:text=Adults%20who%20sleep%20fewer%20than,6.2%20hours.

31. *The Truth About*, episode 8, "Alcohol," produced and directed by David Briggs, 59:00, BBC, 2016.

32. John C. Maxwell, *Put Your Dream to the Test: 10 Questions to Help You See It and Seize It* (Nashville, TN: Thomas Nelson, 2009), xv.

ACKNOWLEDGMENTS

First, I thank my mom, Laura Forbes. Mom, in a world full of moms, I'm grateful you're mine. Thank you for your love and encouragement. You're a blessing, and I love you!

To my daughters, Lindsay and Brianna, I'm incredibly thankful for the rare and special gift of being your mom. You bring such goodness, joy, and laughter to our family and to my life. I dedicate this book to you. I love you both with a full and grateful heart.

To the man who has stood by my side and helped me to raise our two incredible daughters, Terry Marek. Thank you for your encouragement, unconditional love, and unwavering support. I love you and I thank you from the bottom of my heart!

To my daughters' husbands, Jenethan and Adam, thank you for loving my girls. It's every mom's dream for her children to be happy and loved, and I know they have love and happiness with you. You are good men! I'm grateful to have you in our family.

To my grandsons, Adrian, Azia, and Forest, and to all of my future grandchildren, I'm very excited to be your Nana! We're going to have so much fun together. As I write this, I'm smiling just thinking about spending time with you. Know that I love you forever and always.

To my dear friends, Lisa "Bestie" Sanchez, Doug Schneider, Deanna Thomas, Paula Carter, Sandi Grant, and Melissa Annan, you are pure sunshine to my soul! Your friendship means the world to me, and I'm blessed to have each of you in my corner.

To my family, Laura and Murray, Bob and Jo-Anne, Deanna and Ted, Nick, Erin, Courtney and Toby, Jan, Brent and Elisa, Karly, Emma, Dawn and Rick, Melissa, and Jennifer. Family is forever! I appreciate and love you.

To my publishing family at Familius, I knew you were the right publisher for me as soon as I saw your mission: Helping Families Be Happy. Christopher Robbins, founder and president of Familius, thank you for the work you do to make a positive difference in families and for believing in me and in this book. Tina Hawley, my editor extraordinaire, your skill and talent were an invaluable asset to the writing of this book. Thank you for all you did to make sure these pages were the best they could possibly be. To the entire Familius family, an enormous amount of teamwork goes into publishing a book, and I'm thankful for each and every one of you who helped me bring this book into the world!

To my hard-working, loyal, and brilliant editor Katherine Coy, thank you for working on this book with me. You've been editing my work for over fifteen years, and I can always count on you to bring that extra-special something that makes my words shine! To Marisa Solis, thank you for your insight and assistance in developing my book proposal and for staying in my corner until I found just the right publisher for this new book. I'm so thankful! To Jennifer McAuliffe, thank you for adding the perfect amount of "punch" to this book. If laughter is the best medicine, you would make one funny pharmacist! To Jordan Leroux, thank you for your creative eye. You've been my web designer, graphic designer, photographer, and videographer for over a decade—thank you for making me, and my business, look good in print and online!

To Jason Sudeikis, your joy and comedy makes me feel like I fell out of a lucky tree. You make the world brighter! Thank you for giving me your personal two thumbs up (through my awesome cousin Brent Geris, of course) to quote one of your famous lines from Ted Lasso in this book. Everyone else—watch Ted Lasso! Write it in your action plan immediately. Watching this show will make your tummy happy.

To my favorite World Champion Speakers, Darren LaCroix and Mark Brown, thank you for showing me how to make my stories unforgettable. You really blessed me with your time and talent!

And, to you—my readers, Facebook community, loyal subscribers, and students—thank you for allowing me into your life and for giving me a platform from which I can bring CALM to the world to help more moms enjoy the parenting experience with less worry and greater inner peace, so they can raise confident, kind, and happy children.

About the Author

Denise Marek is internationally known as the Worry Management Expert and the creator of the CALM™ methodology for worry-free living. As a lecturer, consultant, and writer, Denise empowers individuals and organizations around the globe to reconnect with their inner peace, overcome their fears, and take the risks that are essential for personal and professional success.

Denise is the author of several books, including *CALM: A Proven Four-Step Process Designed Specifically for Women Who Worry* (Hay House, 2006). She also teaches CALM Online, an online training program that teaches strategies to let go of worry, reduce stress, and create a happier life.

Denise has been awarded the Toastmasters International Accredited Speaker Award for Professionalism and Outstanding Achievement in Public Speaking. She was the first woman in Ontario to have ever received this honor, and fewer than one hundred individuals worldwide have received the Accredited Speaker designation.

Denise lives in Ontario, Canada. She is the mother of Lindsay and Brianna and the nana of Adrian, Azia, and Forest.

For more information on the CALM Online training program, to inquire about speaking engagements, or to sign up for her blog, visit www.denisemarek.com. Follow on Instagram @thedenisemarek and @calmformoms. Follow on Facebook at facebook.com/thedenisemarek. Subscribe on YouTube at www.youtube.com/user/denisemarek.

About Familius

Visit Our Website: www.familius.com

Familius is a global trade publishing company that publishes books and other content to help families be happy. We believe that the family is the fundamental unit of society and that happy families are the foundation of a happy life. We recognize that every family looks different, and we passionately believe in helping all families find greater joy. To that end, we publish books for children and adults that invite families to live the Familius Ten Habits of Happy Family Life: *love together, play together, learn together, work together, talk together, heal together, read together, eat together, give together,* and *laugh together.* Founded in 2012, Familius is located in Sanger, California.

Connect

¤ Facebook: www.facebook.com/familiustalk
¤ Twitter: @familiustalk, @paterfamilius1
¤ Pinterest: www.pinterest.com/familius
¤ Instagram: @familiustalk

FAMILIUS

The most important work you ever do
will be within the walls of your own home.